BEFORE I SLEEP

Before I Sleep

Poetry, Prose, and Peculiarity

LJ Keys

Pantheon of Grace

Published by Pantheon of Grace

Paperback ISBN 978-0-578-93643-7
e-Book ISBN 978-0-578-93644-4

Internal Illustrations by Luc Bardi
Cover Art and Graphic Design by Rob Halhead-Baker
Edited by Stephen Parolini
Proofread by Kraken Editing & Literary Service Investigations

Typesetting services by BOOKOW.COM

Acknowledgments

This book is a gift to myself. It is the culmination of more than three years of full-time therapy, deep reflection, and as many of us have recently experienced, a heaping portion of alone time. I am thankful for the time I've been able to devote to myself and to this process. I'm thankful for Casey, the person who sat with me in the dark and loved me.

This book would also not have been possible without the unending love and understanding constantly poured on me by:

Sally Blanton
Ali Clark
Sarah Makosy
Caitlin McCormick
Darren Harper
Cassie Knab
Amanda Lycett
Emily Putzer
Courtney Kinkel
Jen Thomas
and Alicia Holston

And special thanks to my therapist. Omg, my therapist.

Content Warnings can be found on page 185
for anyone that would like them.

CONTENTS

II   The Garden   53

The Middle   77

III   The Rooms   101

The On-Going   123

IV The Mirror   139

Home   173

Content Warnings   185

Inspirations and Healing   187

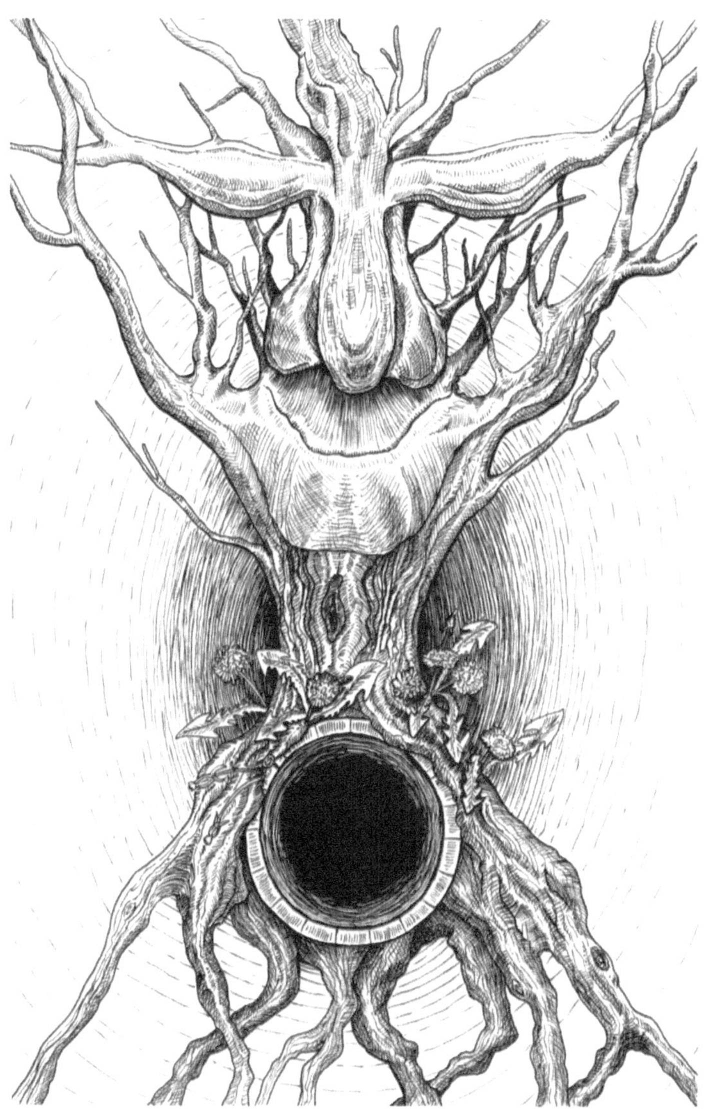

PROLOGUE

I lowered myself into the cave, pausing to adjust my helmet.
My hands were shaking.

I pointed my headlamp downward, feeling the helmet shaking along with my hand.

The descent into darkness always got my adrenaline pumping.

I could feel it circulating along with my blood.

A surge of excitement accompanied each heartbeat.

I released more rope and made yet another mental checklist of the items in my pack.

By the time I reached the ground, I was certain I had everything I needed.

I'd done this before. I knew what to expect.

The cave system was new to me, but I was not alone. My guide greeted me at the bottom as I unharnessed myself.

We directed our headlamps forward and walked toward the largest opening in the rock.

It was early in the day and although the sunlight poured in like rain, it didn't reach the floor.

I glanced up, the green brush at the entrance of the cave barely visible. The sound of flowing water somewhere below, the air thick with moisture.

Triple checking my gear, I nodded that I was ready to go.

We moved forward, slow.

The terrain was rough, but I knew where to step, how not to twist my ankle or to fall.

Thirty minutes passed.

My arms now spanned the width of the tunnel. I tested it.

A claustrophobic caver.

Forty minutes.

I thought about what was above us.

How we would have navigated here if we were above ground.

I asked my guide if we were almost there. Without answering, she waved me on.

We walked another ten minutes before she put her hand up to stop me.

She turned to look at me. I could only see the outline of her face with her headlamp blaring. We stood for a moment. She angled her light away from my face and I saw her smile flood into her eyes.

We crouched down to go a few more steps and

The Earth opened before me.

A cavern the likes of which I'd never seen.

In the darkness, the ceiling rose to some unknown height, the walls to some unknown width.

My breath caught.

It was beautiful. The most beautiful thing I'd ever seen. The shine of the walls, the smell of ancient rock and water. The chill in the air gave me goosebumps. I looked to my guide and she held her hand out before her.

We moved forward, reaching for our flashlights.

Rocks of all sizes littered the ground but just ahead, there was a defined path.

I walked first, my guide following.

The ceiling was too high to see in some places. Even with our flashlights.

But in others, I could see the tips of the hovering stalactites. I was tempted to be afraid.

The air was heavier here. It was so humid, I felt like I was swimming.

As we wandered through the boulders, I ran my hand over one. It was cold and damp. I placed my palm flat against the side, closed my eyes, and pressed. It seemed to warm under my hand.

I think I made a friend.

We continued on for an hour or so until we reached the end of the room. My guide gestured forward.

I looked at her, puzzled.

She pointed toward a small hole near the ground. Made a move that suggested I should look through it.

I knelt, holding up my flashlight, forgetting I was already wearing a headlamp.

I could hear the rushing water.

I got down as low as I could and peered through. The hole was about a foot wide and three feet deep.

I shined my light down the narrow stone tunnel for what seemed like forever. I glanced up at my guide, her earnest eyes urging me on.

Then I caught a glimpse of

Something.

My heart skipped a beat.

My guide smiled reassuringly, offering her hand.

As I stood, I wasn't sure how I felt.

I knew the water was there,

But hearing it rush just behind this wall,

Hearing the force of it?

My hands began to shake again

And my heart fluttered like a bird stuck in a collapsing mine.

Still, I longed to be on the other side.
She knew I did.
But for today, we were done.
This was further than we'd ever gone.
There were many other openings to explore.
Many other ways to get through.
We'd find them.
With a meaningful glance, and a tap of her wrist,
My guide suggested we go.
And we started back toward the sunlight.

Part I

The Woods

WE wake up together, the woods and I.

A single bird sings in the sunrise. The sun peers through the branches, splashing buckets of light on the leaf-covered ground.

There's a vibrant chill in the air. It hastens my step. The breeze carries the smell of rain, mixing with the taste of cinnamon left from my morning tea.

The combination awakens my lungs.

I walk the path I've known for years and feel its familiarity humming in my veins.

The bird song ebbs and flows.

I find him high in the branches of a nearby tree.

I wonder what I look like from way up there.

I wonder what I look like to the squirrels. They chase each other around the trunk and the chipmunks rustle the brush around the roots.

I wonder what I look like to the trees.

Maybe I'm just a passing sound wave, or a scent, or perhaps a color.

The sun rises slow as I come upon the clearing.

Today, the grass sways like a couple cheek to cheek. Deep hues of green and a glitter of lime where the sun hits just right.

Sometimes I come here to celebrate, sometimes to cry, sometimes to scream.

Dandelions pepper the ground, joined by a blanket of forget-me-knots; a bounding blue sea of golden bottle cap ships. I sit amidst them until the sun is high, my neck is warm, and my soul is full.

I find the path out on the other side of the clearing.

The shade of the trees is a welcome break.

But something is different here.

Something intangible. An intuition? A ghost?

I take in the dirt and earth stretching out before me and focus on my feet.

I settle back into the comfort of the woods.

I step over the twisted roots and the occasional downed tree.

My feet carry me of their own volition.

Suddenly, they stop.

The unfamiliar takes the form of a fork in the trail.

Something rises from my belly but I ignore it.

I look down the path to the right.

I look down the path to the left.

I close my eyes.

Breath fills my lungs and holds.

I open one eye. The fork's still there.

My lungs and my sails deflate.

I can't stay here all day.

Decisions. I'm terrible at them.

Eventually, I walk to the right.

Not three steps in, a wash of reassurance douses the flutter in my chest.

I listen to the rhythm of my steps and feel my jaw begin to unclench.

As my shoulders relax, I think about the path to the left.

Was it really there?

The woods break my silent contemplation.

Three deer gracefully bound over roots and brush, sunlight catching the antlers of an enormous buck.

The sudden noise stops me in my tracks.

Curiosity gets the better of me.

I turn on my heels, determined to find the other path.

I walk and walk; sure I've gone far enough.

But I look and look to no avail.

I reach the clearing again. The green grass welcomes me, but it's lost some of its luster.

I must have made it up. There was no other path, no fork, no alternative.

Back down the trail for the second time.

I cross roots and trees when

My feet stop again.

The fork.

The path to the left is still oddly familiar and this time, I take it.

It's just as smooth, just as sun-drenched, just as warm and inviting.

I walk for quite some time before realizing evening is approaching. The sun is still hours from the horizon, but I need to be out of the woods by dark.

Annoyed by how much time I wasted deciding which path to take, I turn around.

The sun is low in the sky when I reach the clearing. The area is bathed in golden light. I say goodnight to my forget-me-nots and dandelions, blowing them kisses.

I make my way toward the path I took in.

But

The path is gone.

I look at the dandelions as if they've betrayed me.

I must have gotten turned around.

I must have made a mistake.

I circle the clearing and find nothing but thick woods and the path to the fork.

The brush has grown thicker along with my saliva.

I swallow hard.

I walk the edge of the clearing two more times finding nothing. I stand in front of the path I've already taken twice today.

I don't have a choice, I think.

I wonder if I've already made one.

I pick some forget-me-nots and put them in my hair before beginning yet another walk down The Trail to Nowhere.

Maybe I'm in a time loop. I laugh, distracting myself from my fists balled tight in my pockets.

In the dim glow of dusk, I reach what used to be the fork.

This time, the path to the right is completely overgrown.

How is this possible? I've been coming to these woods every day for years.

My mind is reeling.

My heart skips a beat as it does from time to time, making me a little lightheaded. My palms are sweaty, my knees are shaking ever so slightly. I lower into a crouch and breathe deep.

The woods look different in the dark.

I reach up to hold my head and feel the flowers I'd put in my hair.

They give me courage.

I listen for life.

I hear the scurry of a chipmunk, distant frogs croaking, and crickets beginning their spirited chorus.

I get up.

My nerves begin to calm.

The moon is rising now.

My feet back on solid ground, I must be moving quickly. I've already reached the place where I'd turned around earlier.

Unknown territory, I think. *From this point forward. Unknown.*

Leaves crunch beneath my feet. I take a few more steps before I recognize it as a new sound.

There's no more trail. The brush thins from this point forward.

I can walk freely through the trees, but I'm much more likely to lose my way without a trail.

It's quiet.

The woods are calm.

As if in response to my thought, I feel tension's hands pressing down on my shoulders.

There's darkness ahead.

Moonlit leaves and tree trunks paint the view behind me but in front, about twenty yards out, I see nothing.

I approach the darkness and it becomes less of a void and more of a thing.

It's a wall.

A wall? There's a wall in the middle of the woods.

The dark stone becomes clear in the moonlight.

The temperature drops as I draw near.

My hand touches the stone, rests flat against the surface.

The chill chases the blood from my hands.

What is this place?

I lean against the wall and let the coolness soak me through.

But I need to know where I am.

I need to get home.

My panic ramps up only to pause and be replaced by something greater.

There is a new silence to the woods. The kind that's so dense, you feel your hearing shift, like your eyes adapting to bright light.

I move away from the wall.

The moonlight brightens just for me to see.

I look up and see the tree branches graze the wall.

I look to my left and then to my right. I look again, hoping the view will change.

I see only darkness, the woods, and stone.

But a wall has to be a good sign, I think. Something is on the other side. Or there will be a gate or it will end.

I should follow the wall.

East or west?

I weigh my options and choose east.

I can't believe I'm lost. I don't get lost!

The woods are scary at night. This sucks. This really, really sucks.

Not above pouting, I dramatically stomp, then walk and eventually meander until I see dawn begin to trickle between the leaves.

I've been out here for twenty-four hours. Twenty-four fucking hours in the woods.

The wall still stretches out before me.

"Hello?" I yell.

"Can anyone hear me?" My voice cracks.

Nothing answers but the wind.

I should have gone west.

Yeah, turn around again. Just keep turning around.

I tell myself not to and yet, I still turn and walk back whence I came.

Around midday, I see my upturned leaves and footprints. I've reached where my path first met the wall.

I don't wanna go west, I whine to myself with a stomp.

I want to go north but there is no way to climb. I punch the wall and hurt my hand.

I'm not even sure I could get back to the southern trail - I kick a tree to the south and possibly break a toe - *and even if I could, I lost the trailhead in the clearing! How is this happening? How did I manage to fuck up a walk in the woods?*

Defeated, I limp west.

I sigh loud enough to scare a bird as I see the sky start to grey with the beginnings of night. The sigh turns into an angry guttural yell. I flail my arms and kick up a flourish of leaves.

I look around the empty woods feeling the full force of the tantrum inside me.

I scream. I scream like I have never screamed before. My temples pulse and my vision blurs. I bellow, feeling the entirety of the scream from its origin inside me to its freedom above me.

I collapse.

The ground catches me with a thud, the jostle shaking loose my tears.

I catch them with the sleeves of my sweatshirt. It smells like home and only makes me cry harder.

I am lost.

I am alone.

I look up at the wall, blurry through my tears. I stare at it hard.

Dirt clumps under my nails as I scrounge the ground for anything – a stick, a handful of leaves, a stone. Whatever I find, I throw at the wall. I throw until my shoulder is sore.

I've stopped crying but the post cry hangover is coming on strong, a dull roar igniting behind my eyebrows.

I lean back until my head rests against the moss and leaves, looking up at what is once again a night sky.

I roll to my side, pulling my knees to my chest, and close my eyes.

At barely a whisper, I ask the wall, "What do you want from me?"

Something changes in the energy around me.

I expect to catch a flash of a white deer tail or a glimpse of a bushy squirrel tail when I open my eyes.

When I do, no more than ten inches from my face

is the face of a little girl.

I scream and shuffle backward on my elbows.

She screams and backs away.

And she starts crying.

She can't be more than five.

I get to my knees, looking around the woods, squinting to see who is here with her.

She's small and wearing pajamas with bright red, blue, and yellow balloons. Grass stains and dirt scuffs splash between the colorful images. I wonder how long she's been out here.

She's on her knees, crying into her hands, quiet as a mouse. She glances at me every few sobs.

Her eyes are pleading, and my heart softens.

"Sweetie," I say, "are you lost?"

"No," she says without looking up.

"Do you live nearby?" I ask.

"Yes," she says as she glances at the wall.

I look at the wall too, hoping to find answers etched in the stone.

"Why are you crying?" I ask.

"Because of… your… your question," she stutters out, crying harder now.

My question?

Without warning, she stands. Frightened by the quick movement, I rush to my feet too. She's still crying as she turns and begins to run. She's running directly at the wall as fast as she can. Adrenaline pumping, I run after her.

"Wait!" I yell.

I'm at least three strides behind her as she reaches the wall.

I hear a body collide with the stone. I hear a skull bounce off it, the sound like a sturdy mug bouncing on linoleum.

It takes me a second to realize it was my skull. My head is throbbing.

I feel the wall where the little girl disappeared…

… through the wall?

I reach up to find a small spill of blood from my forehead.

I can't help but laugh.

I've gone crazy. I knew it would happen. I was honestly just waiting. It was so subtle! But here we are. Chasing after imaginary little girls in the fucking woods.

It's still dark, so I find my mossy patch and sit back down, holding my head. I lie down and close my eyes again. I try not to wonder if I have a concussion.

"What are you playing at?" I ask myself aloud.

"You want to play?" asks the little girl, sitting by my side once more.

"Are you fucking kidding me?" I scream and scramble away from her again.

She looks at me, her shoulders slump forward and her eyes well up.

I sigh.

"I'm sorry," I say.

"You're not sorry," she says with certainty, shaking her little head. Tears hang on the edge of her eyes like small creatures dangling from a cliff.

I get to my knees again, put my hand over my heart, and try to slow my breathing.

She mimics me, hand over her heart.

"I really am sorry. It was very rude of me to yell at you and especially, to swear at you. You just scared me. I'm lost and frustrated. And you seem to have come out of nowhere which scares me even more."

"I didn't come out of nowhere," says the little girl, her face scrunching with concern.

"No, no," I say, reflexively shuffling closer to try to calm her, "I didn't mean you really came out of nowhere. I just mean, I don't know where you came from. And then you were sitting next to me, very close to me, and surprised me!" I made a hand motion along with the word 'surprise'. She smiles but as quickly as it rose to her face, it vanishes.

"I did sneak a little," she admits, looking at the ground.

She maneuvers her feet out from under her and folds into sitting criss-cross applesauce.

I watch her again, waiting.

She begins searching the ground in front of her, sorting pretty leaves, small stones, and pebbles into respective piles.

I move closer.

Now I'm also sitting crisscross applesauce, a couple of feet away from her. We look ready for a game of patty-cake.

"So," I ask, dropping my hands into my lap, "Why are you in the woods?"

"Why are you in the woods?" she asks, mimicking my involuntary hand movements.

"I told you, I'm lost," I reply.

"Me too," she responds.

"Ah, but you told me you weren't lost, remember?" I say.

"Yes –" She seems as if she wants to say more but instead, she goes back to the handful of stones she's collected in front of her.

"And you're in your pajamas!" I say with a brightening face. "I kind of wish I was in my pajamas."

"No, you don't," she says, still curating her rock collection.

"You're a smart little girl," I say.

I don't know what I'm doing. I look around the woods hoping for something to come to me. I see a small heart-shaped rock next to my foot. I pick it up and hold it out to her.

She looks at my palm, then at my face. She holds my gaze and breaks into a slight smile. She takes the stone. Her fingers are warm and solid on my hand.

She is real.

"What's your name?" I ask her.

"What's *your* name?" she asks.

"Ah, I've played this game before," I say with a laugh. "My name is Echo."

"My name is Echo," she says back to me.

"But that's my name!" I say with an animated face.

She giggles.

She puts her hands on the ground in front of her to stand up.

"Wait –" I say, hoping she's not about to run off again.

"I'll be right back!" she says, putting up her hand to suggest I stay where I am. She reiterates, "Right back!"

She's almost out of my sight before she stoops behind a tree. She picks something up and brushes it off.

"Got her!" I hear her little voice echo through the night.

Chills run up my spine.

She makes her way back to me, taking care to step over roots, using the occasional tree trunk for balance.

As she approaches me, the moonlight falls on the item tucked under her arm.

My stomach drops and my head rushes. I force a smile. "Whatcha got there?"

"Dorothy!" she cries.

I recognize the dirt-covered teddy bear.

"Oh my," I say, feeling woozy but still refusing to believe. "Where did you get her?"

"My brother," the little girl says.

My heart races.

She hugs the bear up under her chin, "Once, he put her whole head in his mouth."

I pull myself back a few feet.

She looks confused.

I feel nauseous.

"Where are you going?" she asks, her eyes genuine.

"What's going on?" I ask her.

She's quiet.

"Why are you in the woods? What is this really about?" I ask her again. My voice is shaking.

"I –" she starts and then stops to look at her feet.

"What were you going to say?" I ask. "Say it."

"I don't know!" she says with urgency. She looks like she might cry again.

"You don't know why you're in the woods or you don't know what you were going to say?" I ask.

"I don't know either of those," she says as she looks at the ground in front of her. Her little bottom lip is still pushed out but she's trying so hard to keep from crying.

My heart softens a little.

I scooch toward her again; toward five-year-old me in dirty pajamas, holding a dirty bear, sitting on the ground in the dark woods just before midnight.

"Ok, honey," I say. I'm not sure if the shake of my shoulders is due to the cold or fear. "What's the last thing you remember?"

"I don't feel good," she says.

"What doesn't feel good?" I ask.

"My stomach," she says.

"Your stomach hurts pretty often, huh?" I ask, remembering.

She nods.

"Can you tell me why your stomach hurts?"

She thinks.

"It's just not supposed to."

"Your stomach's not supposed to hurt?" I ask.

She nods again, "I get in trouble."

"For what?" I ask.

"Because my stomach hurts. Or if I'm crying," she says.

"Do you cry a lot?" I ask.

"Yeah," she says, pushing messy strands of hair out of her eyes with a flat palm. It falls back into her face.

"Why do you cry?" I ask.

She plays with Dorothy for a minute, sitting the bear on her knee.

"I'm kind of scared," she says.

"What are you scared of?"

"I don't know," she says.

"Why don't you think about it for a few minutes," I say.

She looks down at Dorothy and straightens the bear's pink, floral dress before hugging it back up under her chin.

"I don't know," she says again but I can tell there's more air in her lungs.

She fidgets, getting uncomfortable.

"It's ok, you can tell me anything," I say.

"You," she whispers.

"Yes, you can tell me anything," I make sure my voice is supportive.

"No, you. You're scary," she says.

My face contorts with confusion.

She sees and her posture changes as if she's somehow getting smaller.

Suspicion and arrogance tense the muscles in my back. *She's scared of me?*

I try to put a smile back on my face before I ask, "What do you mean?"

The hug she's giving Dorothy tightens.

I reach toward her and she backs away.

"Sweetie, why are you scared of me?" I ask, hiding my bemusement.

"You don't think I'm real. You don't…" she trails off.

"Understand?" I ask.

She nods.

With my best understanding voice, I say, "Can you blame me? You showed up out of nowhere and scared me half to death."

She was right. I didn't understand.

She glances at me and then looks back at the stones she has piled in front of her.

We sit like this for a long time.

I look around the woods and draw air deep into my lungs before releasing it back into the wild.

She finally looks back at me. This time, without looking away.

Her focus makes my spine straighten.

I wait.

But she outwaits me.

"Did you want to say something?" I finally ask.

She picks Dorothy back up before nodding.

I lean forward.

"Go ahead."

"You don't…" she drifts off mid-sentence and snuggles Dorothy up under her chin.

"I don't what?" I prod her.

"You don't like when I say it," she says.

I think about how to respond to that. I think back to me as a little girl.

"I think… I think it's important to share how you feel. Even if sometimes, someone doesn't like it. That's not what matters. Saying what you need to is the part that matters most."

"You don't trust me," she says, matter-of-factly.

"Well," I say, "I don't know who or what you are. I don't know what you want from me or what you're going to do to me. So, you're kind of right."

I watch her, thinking she'll burst into tears again or run back through the wall.

But instead, she says, "Why?"

Indignant, I say, "I just told you why."

"But you know who I am," she says.

This time, I fall silent and glance at the ground before looking back up at the little girl.

She is quiet but I watch her posture change again. She sits taller, emotion brimming, boiling over.

"You think you don't know who I am or what I am - but that's the whole point."

Her little hands are shaking now.

I'm tempted to take them in my hands.

"And you left me," she says.

I wait for more but nothing comes.

"I still don't understand," I say.

She sighs, "This is where I come when I'm scared. The woods used to scare me at night so first, I hid Dorothy here so she'd always be with me. Then I made another friend."

She holds my gaze and it feels like someone touches the back of my neck with a cold beer can.

I hear a twig snap behind me and my heart jumps into my throat.

"She's not here. I know when she's here," says the little girl.

"Who is she?" I ask.

"I'm—I'm not sure," says the little girl, "But she doesn't have eyes."

I didn't think my pulse could get faster.

"How does she see?" I ask, looking around the woods.

"She doesn't. She just feels."

"You said that you come here a lot," I begin, "But what makes you come here?"

The silence between us grows louder.

She refuses to look at me.

"What happened the first time you came here?"

She whispers, "You don't remember?"

I hear another twig snap behind me, and I twist to catch the culprit. A breeze rustles my hair. The woods are chilly but the breeze is hot and smells of something old, something rank.

"Now she's here," says the little girl.

I turn my head back and, inches from my skin, I see what must have once been a woman's face.

Time slows.

I can't look away.

It's like the face was once completely blank.

No nose, no mouth, no eyes.

But something carved out where these features would have been.

There is a gaping hole where her mouth should be, but no teeth, no tongue.

The edges around it are caked with scabs, cracked and bleeding.

Her nose is only two small round holes as if poked through with a pencil.

Her eyes.

Her eyes look like they once were like her mouth.

Hanging open.

Open and empty

But now, they are sewn shut, pus oozing between the flesh and string.

She grabs my face and I'm paralyzed. The smell is so strong, I can almost taste it: some rotten mixture of earth, mold, and infection. Still holding my

face, the woman moves to the side, allowing me to see the little girl again. The child shuffles to her feet, puts one hand on the creature's shoulder, and reaches her other hand toward me.

I close my eyes before feeling a small, cold finger press against my forehead. She's gentle, as if touching a flower petal.

The terrible smell is gone. Now only dried leaves and soil fill my nose.

I hear a cricket playing its violin for the first time in hours.

I'm standing.

I open my eyes and release a breath that had been caught between my ribs.

I'm still in the woods

but they are empty.

I was chilled before but now my body aches with an unnatural cold.

I look down. My hands are translucent.

What the fuck, my thoughts move slowly.

I'm shocked back to my surroundings when a scream echoes through the trees. The sound waves are visible to me. They shimmer as they bounce from tree to tree. They pass through me with nothing more than a flutter.

Another scream.

I don't know where to focus my attention. As I examine my translucent body, I realize I have full function of it.

And whether I'm dead or alive, someone is screaming.

I steel myself and run toward where the sound waves seem to have originated.

I find a little girl, the little girl, running through the woods.

But she's even smaller. She looks like she's two.

I run toward her but she can't see me.

She runs with the unsteady gait of a toddler. She comes to a complete stop to look behind her.

She's crying but quiet.

Like she's hiding.

I kneel in front of her.

"I can help you!" I yell as she approaches.

She passes through me

but not before I notice a small knife protruding from her little chest.

That can't be right.

I can't have seen that right.

My stomach is full of pop rocks.

I get up and run after her.

She hasn't gotten far and continues to look behind her every few strides.

I look too but see nothing.

A deep, dense nothing that's closing in.

We've almost made it back to the place we were sitting when I see someone else.

Me.

Maybe a few years younger but a full adult me, approaching the stone wall just as I had days before.

This whole thing has been too much but when I see myself, as I am now, it's like looking in a mirror. I see the distress on her face.

On my face.

Even in my translucent body, I feel the blood drain as my head dives into a pool of overwhelm. I stumble and lean on a tree to stabilize myself. I want to run away.

But I don't.

The little girl must have seen the other me too. She's screaming now.

The Other Me runs toward her and falls to the ground in an attempt to catch the child. The Other holds the little girl. Both are silent.

Like an electric shock to The Other, the child speaks, her two-year-old words muddled by the tears, "Help."

She says it again and again, looking up at The Other's face and then down at her wound.

The Other is shaking, "What happened to —how did this —where did you —." She can't finish a sentence.

She moves a trembling hand toward the small knife. The Other barely touches the handle when the child lets out another blood-curdling scream followed by, "No —no —no," the words broken by sobs.

"I don't know how to help you, sweetheart. Hold on, okay? Just hold on and we'll get you help." Panic sets in as The Other looks around the woods like she's looking for a payphone or the blinding lights of an ambulance.

I hear her muttering, "Fuck, fuck, fuck, fuck," before screaming, "Help! Someone help!"

She screams into the empty woods until her face is red. The child grows even quieter.

"This can't be real, this can't be real," The Other begins chanting as she gently sets the child down on the ground.

I run to the little girl and kneel beside her. I still don't remember this and I'm starting to realize why I might not have wanted to.

The Other continues to back away from us, wringing her hands. She squeezes her eyes closed and opens them wide, still repeating her new mantra.

"This can't be real. This can't be real."

A now familiar stench fills the woods as I see something peer out from behind a tree near the other me. The eyeless creature ambles into full view. She speaks – if you can call it that. It's more like she opens her mouth as wide as it will go and the words emit from her like a sound from an old phonograph, "How dare you retreat."

The other me screams at the sight of the creature. With hasty footsteps, the creature moves toward the other me. The smell overcomes the Other and she pukes into the leaves at her feet.

"Please, please don't hurt me —there's a child, she's hurt, I need to help her," The Other pleads.

"So, now you want to help her?" the creature speaks on the wind as I watch her words swirl around The Other like a small tornado.

"I —I don't know how," says The Other.

"And so, you leave her here," says the creature, motioning to the dark woods.

"No, I —," The Other started.

The creature moves toward her again and The Other rushes backward. The Other glances at the child once more. And I feel what happens next before I see it.

And remember. Like a bad dream.

The Other whispers, "I'm sorry," before running away, through the woods. The faster she runs, the louder her thoughts bleed into my consciousness: *I'm sorry, I'm so sorry. This isn't real, I'm so sorry, this isn't real, this can't be real —*

It isn't long before my transparent hands are shaking just as The Other's had been. I scoop the air, trying to pick up the child but passing through her.

The child, growing more and more still by the minute, whimpers as the creature approaches.

I stay at her side, still trying to scoop her into my arms and run away with her. Take her somewhere safe.

The creature kneels beside her too.

"Hush now, child, hush. I am here, I will always be here," she says.

The creature picks up the child and before heading deeper into the woods, glances in my direction.

Chills shoot down my arms, setting off fireworks in my fingertips.

I try to follow but they round one tree and then another.

And then they're gone as if through a magic door cut into a tree trunk. My vision begins to fade.

I close my eyes again and brace myself for what's to come.

Earth and dried blood. Bacteria and pus. The smell is hot in my nostrils.

I open my eyes, still paralyzed, my head in the creature's hands and the little girl's finger drawing back from my forehead.

The creature releases me and backs away, standing behind the little girl, hands resting on her little shoulders.

The girl looks into my eyes.

For the first time, I feel her anger.

"You. Left me," she says.

I am quiet. I struggle to breathe with the scent of the creature hanging so close by but the child seems immune.

"I —I am so sorry," I say, looking at my hands. I'm surprised to feel my face flush and my eyes water.

The girl and the creature wait for me to continue.

"I thought it was a dream. I didn't even remember it until you," I glance at the creature. "I didn't know it was real, I swear I didn't know it was real."

The creature opens her mouth and words rush toward me, circling above my head like vultures, "What is real?"

I look from the creature to the girl and back again. "I'm still not sure."

The creature starts toward me, but the girl holds up her hand.

The child looks up at the eyeless face. "I think we're okay now."

The creature nods before making its way back into the woods.

The little girl seems older than before.

Maybe it's just the patchy moonlight playing a trick.

"What is real?" she asks me again.

"I —I don't know," I say, feeling like a child myself. I avoid the teacher's eye contact, hoping she won't call on me again. It doesn't work.

"This is real to me." She places her hand on the trunk of a tree. "This is real." She holds Dorothy out to me. I take the teddy bear. "This is real," she says as she pulls down the neck of her balloon pajamas so I can see the place where she'd been stabbed.

"Oh, sweetie." I get to my knees and shuffle toward her. The wound is infected. Her skin is hot near the cut and green pus oozes from a small opening at the base of a jagged scar. It's beginning to smell like the creature. I feel her forehead. She's burning up.

"She didn't treat this?" I ask.

"She taught me how to ignore it," says the little girl with a reassuring voice.

"Sweetie, you need to go to a doctor," I say. "I won't make the same mistake twice. Come with me."

I stand and look around the woods again. My heart is still racing. I feel a little faint.

I put out my hand for the little girl to hold but no one grabs it.

Instead, she lies down in the leaves, her clothing now soaked through with sweat.

I kneel at her side. "No, sweetie, come on. We need to get you help."

"You're here now," she whispers.

"I don't know how to help you." I take her hand.

"Yes, you do," she says.

I look around the woods once more as if something might have changed. I see the wall.

"The wall! You ran through the wall—how did you get through?"

"I... I don't know..." She closes her eyes.

"No, sweetie, stay here, stay with me. Tell me how you get through the wall," I ask again, kneeling to hold her little face in my hand.

"I just do," she says, fading.

"Ok," I say. "Then we just will."

I carefully pick her up, cradling her close to my chest.

The smell of the wound is strong. I glance over my shoulder to see the creature half-hidden by a tree.

I break into a run toward the wall.

A sickening scream behind me gives my feet wings.

Twenty feet from the wall, ten feet, five feet.

The screaming stops.

I hear myself panting, smell roses and hear, ever so faint: Johann Sebastian Bach's Prelude No.1 in C.

THE BEGINNING

Self-Portrait

I am a happy girl.
Just ask anyone.
I smile
and laugh
Bright as the sun.

I'm awake
and present
Just look and see!
I'm alive
and real.
What else would I be?

Invisible Pain

The symptoms sink their teeth
The blue jay sings his song
My fingers turn to claws
But I smile and sing along

As the sun shines on my cheeks
A shadow lingers near
When I grab my favorite sun hat
Demons whisper in my ear

I try to call for help
But only sonnets sound
Quietly, I anguish
The moon shines brightly down

A summer breeze through windows
A chill in my bones
Cozy blankets and hot cocoa
I've never felt more alone

Missing

Among the pine trees, I softly skip
Heart rate rising as I almost trip
I catch myself on what must be
The finest, tallest, strongest tree
In the wood.

I gaze upward as if in a trance
I wish to fly to its highest branch
I wish I could go back in time
Back on the ground, I hear you sigh
Next to me.

I heard you wish on that shooting star.
Ask to forget what we've kept so far
From our thoughts, almost forgotten.
My dress made of the softest cotton.
Your hand in mine.

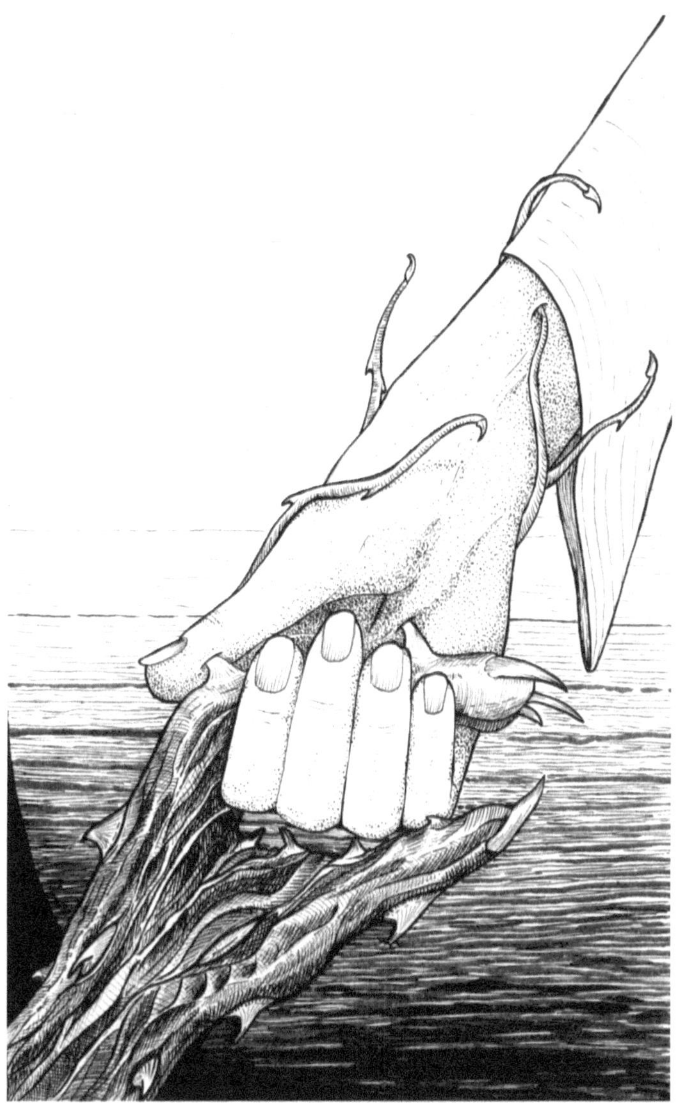

Nothing

The vase fell off the table,
it was no one's fault.
It broke into so many pieces,
small, tiny pieces.
The dust of them just blew away.
I didn't even have to clean it up.
The thing that was once there is now gone.
Or was it ever there?
Maybe I just had an awareness
that most people have a vase.
Maybe I got a table that could hold a vase
and had that table so long
that I forgot I never had a vase.
But then, I've seen its shadow.
It was dark and I tripped.
I flailed and caught myself,
hand pressed hard on the edge of the table.
Out of the corner of my eye, I saw the vase
teeter, wobble, topple.
Fall from sight.
I heard the shatter.
But I've never had a vase.

Is Real

I wake with a start,
My heart
Running a race
Against itself.
What woke me?
I look around
See a shadow
In the corner.
A black silhouette
Against the white wall.
A woman?
She screams.
I wake with a start,
Standing in the corner
Of my bedroom.
Backlit by the night
Light hanging
From the bathroom plug.
I scream.

Shadows

The brick wall,
Your dark silhouette.
Fingers and lips,
Half-smoked cigarettes.
Memories, like faces,
I tend to forget.

In the Core

I'm so afraid.
"Of what," they ask.
"Of nothing."
"Then why are you afraid?" they ask.
"Because there's so much nothing."

Where Do You Go?

To the windmills, I would go.
To connect my mind and soul.
Drive for hours on end.
Savoring each road bend.

Not a soul for country miles,
Only captivating country wiles.
Something in the warm breeze
Would put my fitful heart at ease.

Every trip, the stillness grew
While chasing the morning dew.
To the windmills, I would go.
Driving fast, thinking slow.

Spooning

The dishwasher is full.
Two spoons left.
One big, one small.
"I like the little one," he thinks
And hands her the small spoon.
"I like the big one," she thinks,
"He must not love me."

BFFs

We sit upside down on couches
And imagine
Our feet in the clouds.
Popcorn kernels fall from our eyes
Popping before they hit the ground
Like firecrackers
Set to the frequency of our laughter.
Our fists hold the crumpled fabric
Of the backs of our shirts
So we don't lose each other in the crowd.
We watch Ghosthunters
While we hunt our emotions
But it was just water in the pipes.
We know the things other people wonder.
We use our wonder as a balm
For our dry, cracked skin.

Reunion

The night was Halloween.
The year, not so long ago.
The moon playing hide and seek
When into the graves we strolled.

We didn't see any ghosts
Because we brought our own.
Click, click, click,
Before the lighter shone.

We moved away from there
And they took down the fence.
But still stood those stones.
Two words without pretense.

Youth in the face of death,
Death in place of sadness.
That night, we met our parents
And chased away the madness.

Sure as hell, when we returned
After so many wild years,
Decided to meet in the graveyard
To remember our childhood fears,
We crossed the great, wide country
And there lie Mother and Father.
We thank them for our friendship.
Our mascara runneth over.

A Sad Attempt

Melancholy jollity
A point we turn our heads with ease
Cheerful despondence
Our ears are victims of false pretense
Words upon the crumbling page
Spoken by a sage
As she's stumbling away
A fresh coat of paint on ancient walls
A sad attempt to cover signatures
On the ceiling.

Confident uncertainty
We raise our voices, faults unseen
Enthusiastic ignorance
Our lips are victims of indifference
Actors on the stage
Bumbling
Screaming our age
As we fumble with our prey
One last step before the dancing ends
A sad attempt to remember our friends
Without revealing ourselves.

My Molasses Cookies

and other things I'm good at

Melted margarine
Refined sugar
A beaten egg
Mixed smooth
Sand after a wave

Cloves remind me
Of Christmas
Ground ginger
Yellow raindrops
On white flour

Cinnamon smells
Like Big Red gum
Filling my kitchen
With the spiced smoke
Of a memory

Molasses slips
Out of my hands
Broken glass
Prismed pool
Of day-old blood
Slipping
Down grout lines
Or seeping up

I am also under
The kitchen floor
Reaching through
Sticky sugar and tile
A corpse oozing
Sweet hot sludge

Holding my own ankle
Struggling to write
Poems on the kickboards
Where only I will see

About time wasted
And pretending
I'm wasted
On non-alcoholic
Wine spritzers

Mixing and baking
My legendary cookies
Using Susan's recipe
From Pinterest

Part II

The Garden

STRANDS of small white lights materialize out of thin air. They hang between tall wooden posts, lighting a path through a vibrant garden.

I hug the little girl closer to me and feel her soft breath on my neck.

She's not as warm as she was.

I keep my eyes up, my racing heart keeping me alert like a deer in hunting season.

Behind me, the wall stands whole, firm, and cold.

I hear each note of Bach's Prelude cutting through the night air, meeting my ears as if they are the final stop of a train. I feel each chord shift pulling somewhere deep in my gut like a string tangled in my intestines.

I follow it.

I walk along the path, taking in the bright purple wisteria trees and weeping cherry trees. Pink hydrangeas and coral azaleas line the path. Double roses the size of my hands cupped together sit behind them. Their petals blend fuchsia, red, and crimson.

I smell lilacs.

I reach a break in the foliage as the song ends and another begins. I'm close enough to hear the soft grind and pop of an old record player.

The gravel underfoot turns to stone as I step onto a mosaic patio. Even in this dim light, the lush green of the ivy-covered pergola is stunning. The corner closest to me is held up by the most beautiful statue I've ever seen.

A young woman, tall and strong. One hand is upstretched, holding a corner of the wooden roof. The other hand reaches down toward the ground as if to conjure the stone flames that rise around her. She shines with browns, reds, whites, and oranges. They mix and sway, as frantic as fire. But the woman looks at home amidst the blaze.

I walk around the edge of the pergola to find another statue. Her stone is a rich blend of browns and golds. She's radiant. Both her arms reach upward, fringed with feathers like a great raven.

Still looking for any sign of life, I continue to circle the pergola.

The third statue is even more surreal. She is carved in what looks like wood but it's smooth like stone. Her skin, textured like bark, makes her look like something out of a fairytale. Her hands stretch up into carved leafing branches, her stone legs burrow into the ground like roots, and her stone eyes follow me.

The last statue on the last corner is a lush dark blue with splashes of orange. She is made of stone but might as well be water, the way her dress flows around her like waves cresting and crashing. She holds up the roof just like the others, but her hands look like they were thrown up in a fit of joy. She faces the sky.

Under the pergola sits an ornate metal table and two matching chairs. The record player sings from across the space, on another small table surrounded by potted plants and seedlings just beginning to sprout.

I hear a metallic clatter behind me as well as a sound of surprise. Not quite a scream and definitely not a word.

I jump and turn around to see an elderly woman bent over with her hands on her knees.

"You scared the bejesus out of me," she laughs as she stands back up. She holds her heart for a moment but continues with an unexpected friendliness, "And you are?"

White hair, in a bun on top of her head, draped in an elegant, almost medieval floral robe that sweeps the ground. A small copper watering can on the ground in front of her.

"Please help us," I say, my voice sounding much calmer than I am.

"Help with what?" the old woman asks.

"She's sick, she needs a doctor," I say, looking down at the child in my arms. "Do you have a phone? We should call an ambulance."

The old woman hesitates before smiling, the kind of smile that warms like the heat off an apple pie fresh from the oven. She approaches.

"I don't think she needs an ambulance," she says, her hands hovering over the little girl's back. "All that's left to do is let her go."

I can't believe my ears.

"Let her go?" I ask, flabbergasted.

I hug the little girl tighter.

"It's just an infected wound, she's not gonna die," I say.

The old woman bends to pick up the watering can.

As she stands, she says, "I never said she'll die. But you do have to let her go."

"If you won't help us, can you at least tell me how to get out of this garden?" I ask, impatient.

"No," she says.

"We don't have time for this," my anger rises.

I glance down at the little girl.

Her eyes are closed but the color in her cheeks has returned.

I look back at the old woman and she gestures as if to say, "See?"

I found her. I must help her. I can't let her go again.

"I'll just have to find someone else to help," I say to the old woman as I look for a path on the other side of the pergola.

"Wake up, child. It's no time for sleeping," the old woman's voice whispers in my ear. Chills race from the base of my skull to my neck and dance across my shoulders.

Fear mingles with the muddy water of my anger.

The old woman is not close enough to have whispered like that.

She's nowhere to be seen.

The chill in my shoulders makes its way to my feet and I break into a run.

I head for a path on the other side of the patio and hate the stones and their loud crunch.

I round a corner of tall rose bushes and find myself in a densely packed corridor of white birch trees.

I only notice the lack of music because of the ear-popping silence.

The quiet is so intense that it makes my head spin.

I feel like I've walked through a psychedelic cloud, emerging with the gift of sloth instead of enlightenment.

As I watch a mosquito fly past my face in slow motion, the old woman comes into focus behind it, rounding the far corner. Her illuminated eyes cast a bluish glow down the row of trees. Her beauty strikes me.

"Let her go," her voice echoes.

Her eyes cast strange shadows that dance on the periphery of my vision.

She floats toward me, her robe no longer touching the ground.

I try to move but the harder I try, the slower I go.

I close my eyes and hug the child under my chin as if she were a teddy bear.

I hear the sway of fabric as the old woman draws near.

"Child," the woman whispers.

I hesitate, my hands sweaty. A tear squeezes its way out before I finally open my eyes. I meet hers and I see the moon reflected in them before my head is thrown backward, my neck bending toward my back.

For the briefest moment, I wonder if she shot me.

I stumble but manage to keep hold of the child.

The old woman is still hovering, her robe rippling in conjured air. My hands are shaking but I'm no longer moving in slow motion.

I run.

As soon as my back is to the old woman, shapes form in front of me like holographs.

My eyes are now illuminated with the same bluish hue. But if I move my head, the image disappears.

I reach up to find two holes in the back of my head.

My thoughts go fuzzy, and my knees give way. I do my best to hold onto the child as I fall.

I manage to hold onto consciousness.

On the ground before me, I see a small blue version of myself. It's from the day before I came to the woods. I'm crying and alone. Or I thought I'd been alone.

On the bed next to me, curled against my back, is the little girl.

She sits up and leans over my side, brushing the hair out of my face, wet with tears.

I watch as the images speed up and the little girl brings me things to make me feel better.

Old cartoons, ice cream, popcorn, her baby blanket.

All her favorite things.

Eventually, I get up and leave the bedroom.

She stays on the bed.

She is alone. She is truly alone.

The corridor of trees grows dark again, only the moon and twinkle lights casting their shadows.

I can hear my breath in the silence. Short and choppy.

My chest hurts.

I finally hear a rustle behind me.

The old woman touches my shoulder.

For just a moment, all fear, all fatigue, all confusion is gone. I feel the gentle pressure on my shoulder lighten. I forget myself and wish for the hand to come back. Her voice, like a teabag in hot water, steeps into me.

"She has been and always will be with you. You know that now. And you can't unknow what you know."

I am still and pull the little girl close to me.

Her hair smells of dirt, sunshine, and some vague sweetness. Her skin is soft and rosy.

"Yes," the old woman continues, "she was alone for a long time. She is young and forgives easily. You will never be parted again. But you must let her go."

The old woman brushes past me and the scent of lavender fills my nostrils.

It travels up and up, swirling just behind my forehead, calming with each inhale.

I lean the child away from me for the first time since entering the garden.

She's awake. Her green eyes are vibrant. Her expression is calm and light.

"I'm okay," she tells me.

I help her stand, rising to my knees to meet her. She feels her scar.

Realization washes over her like a waterfall. Her face is the universe, and her eyes, the stars. Happiness pours from her and she hugs me. She hugs me tighter than I thought her little arms could squeeze, with more intention than a hundred souls.

The old woman is right. I'll have this hug with me always. I'll have her with me always.

She releases me and to my surprise, runs to the old woman. The little girl pulls down her collar to show the old woman her healed wound.

"Right as rain," smiles the old woman. "Now why don't you take those little chicken legs on up to the house? You can feed the cats before you go home."

Before I can process all that has happened, the child is gone.

I still feel her presence.

A hand reaches toward me.

With hazy eyes, I follow the arm up to the old woman's face.

Fear comes crashing back down on me like a house collapsing under too much snow.

I shuffle backward, away from her.

She is silent, her hand still outstretched.

I gaze into her face, trying to understand. Even with her years, her skin is smooth like one of her statues. Her eyes no longer glow. I raise my hand to the back of my head.

"They're gone," she says.

I pause at her words but continue to feel my skull for the two holes I'd found just moments ago.

It starts to settle in, how exhausted I am.

My arms and legs are heavy.

The exhaustion is only eclipsed by anger.

I can't even formulate a sentence yet.

"It was necessary," says the old woman, with a kind voice.

"Scaring the shit out of me was necessary?" I manage to say.

"Sometimes we can't reach a place of healing without exhaustion, or without giving something up. Though we don't really give up anything that is a part of us," says the woman.

I don't understand.

The old woman walks toward me. "You will."

She offers her hand again and I take it.

"Up we go," she says. "Come. I have tea."

I follow her, my mind still in a state of disbelief.

We reach the pergola and the record player sings Eric Satie's Gymno-pedie No.1 like a lullaby.

The metal table now has tea for two resting upon it.

The old woman takes a seat and gestures to the one across from her.

I slump into the chair and am surprised by how comfortable the cold metal is.

My eyes focus on the tea set and my breath catches in my throat.

"So, what now?" I ask.

She laughs and waves her hand, "You came to visit me."

My brain feels like it's trying to navigate a dense fog.

She pours the tea.

"Have a sip, sweetheart," she says, passing me a cup and saucer with pink and red strawberries painted on, a familiar crack down one side.

The tea is the kind of warm you can trace down your throat and into your belly where it swirls like cream in coffee.

My shoulders loosen.

It was made perfectly. Mango, ginger, and a whisper of honey.

"Two whispers," says the old woman, "You've had a hard day."

I set the cup down harder than I intend and wince at the clang. I know how fragile it is.

I cross my arms and make eye contact with the old woman. My neck hurts again.

She takes another sip of her tea.

I'm not talking to you, I think.

She leans back and folds her hands, placing them in her lap. Still, she is open and inviting.

I think I'd like to say something and before I can hide the thought away again, she says, "Then speak."

"I broke this cup when I was young," I say, pointing to the teacup. "I get it. The little girl was me when I was little, you're me when I'm old."

"A wise, learned woman in her prime, you mean? Perhaps," she leans forward as she speaks.

"Or you're a witch. Can read my mind?" I ask.

"Close enough," she says.

I don't want to be here, I think.

"Don't you?" she asks.

Why would I want any of this?

"You chose the path," she says. "The fork. In the woods."

Maybe it's the near-euphoric exhaustion, maybe she put something more than honey in the tea, but I laugh.

"So, you're saying that all this happened because I chose a different path in the woods than I walk every week? I tried to go back," I say.

"The path wasn't there, and then it was. You took it. You can't unknow what you know," she repeats.

I feel the little girl hugging me again.

"Would you really want to?" she asks.

I don't speak. I try not to think.

"Take another sip of tea," she says.

Again, the tea slides down into my stomach, soothing each muscle it passes. I close my eyes and relax into the chair.

When I open my eyes, hers are on me. I feel like I've had a full night's rest.

"Better?" she asks.

"Enough with this stuff," I say with force, gesturing at the air as if we're surrounded by magic.

She holds up her hands in surrender but her smile does not fade.

I sigh.

"So, what? Am I supposed to learn something from you too?" I ask.

"Like a parlor trick?" She snaps her fingers and a short burst of fire appears above her hand.

"I literally just said enough of that shit," I say, though my eyes are wide.

I've always liked magic. Ever since I was little.

She laughs and sets a small metal contraption on the table.

"It's a finger flasher," she explains. She picks it up, shows me where to add the flash cotton, places it back in her hand, and makes a motion like she's snapping. She snaps the fingers on her other hand while she flicks the ignition on the toy.

"Tada," she says with another burst of flame.

I've been wavering back and forth between whether this is real, fake, or somewhere between. Now, I'm certain I'm dreaming.

A dream from which I'll wake and create a beautiful work of surrealism.

"Do you wanna try," she asks.

My face scrunches up before I can stop it.

Real, fake, dream, in between...

"Does it matter?" she asks.

I sigh again and extend a clammy hand.

She places the toy on my finger and hands me a bit of the flash cotton from the pocket of her robe.

I stuff it into the small metal cylinder.

"Go ahead," she says, her eyes full of child-like joy.

With a click that sounds like a lighter, a small plume of fire rises from my hand. I feel the heat on my fingers and face but it doesn't burn or pinch.

"Well done! You did forget to snap with your other hand, but once you've mastered that," and she holds her hand flat in front of her. Like a meerkat sticking its head out of a hole, a small flame appears in the middle of her palm and stays there.

I'm dreaming.

The old woman lets out a hearty laugh that makes me think the sun has risen.

"Sweet girl, I know there is nothing I can say to put you at ease, but would you permit me to show you something else?" she asks.

I hesitate.

"No more fire, I promise," she says.

I feel the edges of my mouth begin to curve but stop them.

She extends her hand toward me again.

I look at it and back at her.

She raises her eyebrows and flexes her hand to show I should take it.

I reach out and place my hand on top of hers.

A sensation not unlike the tea in my stomach travels up my arm and gathers in my chest.

I'm no longer afraid. I'm overwhelmed by feelings of love, belonging, and grace.

I bring my other hand to my chest and can feel vibrations emanating outward. They shake lose something in me and my eyes well.

The woman also places her other hand over her heart.

"I just wanted to let you see," she says.

"This is you?" I ask. "This is your heart?"

"Yes," she says.

"It's beautiful," I respond.

The sensation starts to fade and I already miss it.

I pull my hand away just in time to wipe tears before they fall.

"More tea?" her question brings me back to the pergola and the metal chair.

I nod.

When I look back down at the table, a deck of tarot cards has appeared beside the teapot.

"What do you think? Will you humor an old woman?" she asks.

"No," I say.

Her eyes sparkle.

"But a wise, learned woman in her prime? Sure," I continue.

She smiles and begins to shuffle.

The record player has long stopped playing. Now, all I hear is the faint call of crickets, the rustle of ivy in the breeze, and the rhythmic shamble of the tarot cards.

She places the deck before me and I cut it. She puts the halves back together and draws a card.

My throat goes dry.

Death.

"Have another sip," says the woman, pushing my tea toward me.

I do as I'm told but I'm too distracted to notice any calming effects.

I feel drawn into the upside-down picture on the card. The hooded figure sits on stone, one skeletal hand on his hip and the other keeping the hood from covering the empty eye sockets of his skull. Like a gothic Rodin's The Thinker. At Death's feet, there is a weeping woman, a grieving woman.

"Why do you fear this card?" the woman asks, breaking my trance.

"Doesn't everyone fear death?" I ask.

"No," says the woman.

She places her hand on the card, "Death is but a transition, a transformation."

My eyes roll.

The old woman chuckles so her shoulders bounce.

"I'm sorry," she laughs, "Just that eye roll."

I shift in my seat, "Sorry."

She relaxes into her chair, "I know, nothing is as it seems."

"You keep trying to explain away fear," I say.

She raises her eyebrows like I've said something of note.

"What, you're not scared of anything?" I ask.

She contemplates before answering, "I have learned that most of my fears originate within myself. They are created and spread all within my own mind. As such, I do experience fear, but with understanding. So, don't have to be afraid of the fear itself."

My gaze floats back down to the tarot card and I lean forward. The closer I look, the less frightening the card appears. The large skeleton could even be protecting the woman.

"The Death card comes with a lot of misconceptions. Maybe think more about it as the death of something less literal. What has changed in your life?"

"Everything. Always," I say. And then add, "Nothing. Ever."

I take another sip of tea.

She continues, "Well, I think you're here because change is coming. You're in the cocoon, holding the walls tight to your body. You're going to have to come out of there at some point."

I cross my arms over my chest.

The woman clicks her tongue and places her hand back on the tarot deck.

She draws the Strength card. Also reversed.

To my surprise, she lets out a high-pitched squeak before saying, "This is one of my favorites! You've gotta train your lions!"

The picture on the card is beautiful. A woman sits with a white sheet around her like a gown. Her hair is made of flowers and her face is serene. By her knees, a lion sits with its front paws together, his mane flowing around his face like waves. He rests his head against the woman's legs and she rests her hands on his head.

A nudge at my elbow. Before I can cower, a large, pink, bristled tongue scrapes the full length of my face, leaving a trail of moisture.

I nearly fall as I struggle out of the chair.

The big cat does not follow me but instead makes its way to the old woman. She opens her arms as it approaches and it snuggles into her chest. I hear a low rumble. Lions don't purr. They can't. But their sighs seem to harmonize as she whispers to him.

I look around for any idea of what to do.

My hands are shaking again and I feel sweat on my forehead.

Soon, the lion departs, taking the same path the little girl had taken "up to the house".

As soon as it's out of sight, I gawk at the old woman, my face incredulous.

"My lions are tame," she replies.

"Plural?" I yell, looking around the garden.

"Sit down, child," the old woman says in a stern voice.

I return to the chair like a rambunctious child scolded by the teacher.

She moves her hand toward me but does not touch me, "Eureka is my only real lion. The rest are metaphorical."

I gaze at the upside-down strength card while I catch my breath.

"Tell me about your lions," she breaks my trance again.

My heart rate still hasn't regulated.

You can read my mind, you tell me, I think.

"I can't read what isn't written," she says. "Think of lions as the things about yourself that you consider to be, for lack of a better way to say it, too much. Things that you are self-conscious about, that you've been criticized for."

I've barely had a chance to think when I hear her exclaim, "Yes!"

I jump, "What?"

"I heard you whisper it," she says.

"I didn't say anything," I say.

"No, no," she taps her temple.

"Little invasive," I say.

"Sweet thing, you are never more seen than in the presence of yourself," she says.

The statement makes me uncomfortable at first but as it washes over me, it feels like a tidal wave washing something away.

"You said, 'sensitive'," she says.

"Lots of people tell me I'm too sensitive," I say.

"That's a lion. That is not a bad thing and it is not a fault," she says.

I mull it over.

"No matter who says it is," she continues.

I sigh again.

"Untamed, it might take off a head or two," she chuckles, "But tamed, it is a vast strength."

"Last one," she says as she places her hand back on the deck.

She draws The High Priestess. Also reversed.

The cards are all embellished with gold, but this one stands out. Two pillars rise from the bottom of the card, creating a golden archway. Under it, or perhaps a part of it, a woman stands tall. She wears a cornucopia of flowers in her hair and her chin is held high. She wears drapings that look as if they contain stars. In her hands, she grasps a golden book. Her eyes are sure.

"One word: intuition," says the old woman.

I am quiet and don't meet the old woman's gaze.

"You think avoiding my eyes will keep you from owning your gift? I don't need to draw this out of you. It is already there, bubbling below the surface, ready to shoot out of your fingertips.

You wouldn't feel this way if you didn't already know it was there," she says.

"I feel things, sure. But how am I supposed to know what I should be feeling?"

"What does 'supposed to' mean?" she asks.

"How do I know what's real?" I ask.

"Does it matter?" she asks.

I roll my eyes again.

LA PAPESSE

"Does it?" she repeats, doubling down.

"Um, yeah, kinda," I say, my eyebrows rise to meet the mockery in my voice.

"Why?" she asks.

I close my eyes and take a deep breath.

"Child, if this is a dream or this is real, will you still have learned something?" she asks.

"If I remember it," I say.

"It seems to me, your intuition is another lion," she says.

We each take another sip of tea.

"They're all upside-down. Doesn't that mean something?" I ask.

"Yes and no," she says. "The reading still suggests that a change is coming, you have some lions to tame, and you need to learn to trust yourself. The reversal means you are struggling to let go of something, your lions need attention, and... well, that last one stays the same. We're never done learning about intuition."

"So, I'm a mess, yeah, I know. What's new?" I feel something building in my chest that reminds me of high school.

"What is this? What are you feeling?" she asks.

"I have gone through all this to be yelled at?" I ask.

"You're not being yelled at. You took the path. You might not have known how hard it would be but here are your guidelines," she gestures to the three-card spread.

"And how am I supposed to accomplish those things?" I ask.

She furrows her brow. "What do you mean?"

"I don't know how to do all that. I don't understand any of this," I say, feeling my heart flutter with a palpitation.

"All you need to do is stand up and walk around the table," she says, standing.

"It's not that easy," I say.

She smiles before shooing me out of my seat and into hers. She sits across from me and moves our teacups so they follow us to our new seats.

"Are they reversed now?" she asks.

"Well, no... but now they're reversed for you," I say.

"I have been around this table too many times to count," she says. "I don't mind it. Sitting too long looking in one direction can get stagnant. We don't grow if we stay in small pots," she says, motioning to the seedlings next to me.

"So how do you get back to this side?" I ask.

She chuckles again.

"Sometimes you must fight, and learn, and heal. Sometimes the awareness is all you need," she says.

We sit in silence again.

"Let's walk," says the old woman.

"Where?" I ask.

"In the garden," she says, rising and walking away from me.

* * *

Past the hall of birch trees, we come to the furthest corner of the garden. Set back in a grove of greenery is a stone well.

"Speaking of intuition, mine said to bring you here," she says.

The well looks slightly lopsided and is covered in moss. There is no crank to wind the rope to the top. Instead, the long rope is coiled in a pile on the edge of the stacked stone circle, a large bucket on the ground.

"Why did you bring me here if you know I'm afraid of wells?" I ask.

"I don't ask the questions. I just listen. What are you feeling right now?" she asks.

"Like I want to run away," I say.

"But you aren't running. Why?" she asks.

I stay quiet, the image of the well burning itself into my memory.

"Listen to yourself," she says. "Listen deeper than the fear."

"I... I feel like I should look into it. But I don't want to," I say.

She is quiet. She's quiet so long that it becomes apparent she's waiting me out.

I walk toward the well. With each step, I feel my muscles tense. I'm holding my shoulders so tight that they begin to shake.

I stand tall next to it before bending to look in.

The air is damp and heavy with the faint scent of mold and rain.

I place my hands on the stone.

The moisture soaks my fingertips like condensation on glass.

I close my eyes and take a deep breath.

I contemplate running back to the pergola and the calming tea.

But I feel it in my gut. The need to look.

I lean over the edge. The first thing I see is the other side of the well shooting downward. I was hoping I wouldn't have to bend this far to see the bottom. When I'm bent far enough to look directly down, I still cannot see the bottom.

All I can see is the stone cylinder, continuing down and down and down into darkness.

A trick of the light makes it look like the well is spinning counterclockwise.

My eyes adjust and I see, near the edge of where everything turns to black, a glimmer.

Vertigo overcomes me.

"No, no, no, no," I say, backing away from the well, flailing for a handhold.

"Do not panic, sweet girl. It's only stone, water, and earth," says the old woman.

"No, there's something else down there," I say.

The old woman puts her hand on my back, comforting me.

"What do you feel?" she asks.

"I can't," I say, choking back what would be tears if I wasn't so scared.

"Can't what?" she asks.

"Go down there," I say.

She is quiet but stands with me for what could have been five minutes or what could have been an hour. She rubs my back rhythmically. I think about the light I saw. What could it be?

"Why does it have to be the thing I'm most afraid of?" I ask.

"It's the thing you're afraid of because you're afraid of it. Would it even be worth it otherwise?" she asks.

I cast her a glare.

"Fear isn't always a reason not to do something. I know you're nervous. But I'm here," she says. "And you will do what is right."

Without warning, a tear forms and rolls down my cheek. Those words have been said to me before, but they meant more coming from her. From me.

I hug her around the waist.

Eventually, I pull away from her and walk back toward the well, each step unveils a new trauma. Each step is insurmountable until I take it.

When I look over the edge this time, the light has gotten brighter. There's a hole in the wall. I can't tell how big it is from this high up.

"If I wanted to, how would I get down there?" I ask, peering back over the edge.

The old woman puts two of her fingers together, puts them to her lips, and whistles the loudest whistle I've ever heard. Eureka bounds around the corner.

Together, the old woman and I uncoil the rope, giving one end to Eureka who already knows his task. He pulls the line taut as the old woman situates the bucket on the inside wall of the well.

I get in.

"This is dumb," I say.

She laughs knowingly.

"I'm in a bucket," I say.

"Yes, you are. Because you felt you should be," she says.

I roll my eyes.

"Ah, one more eye-roll for the road," she laughs.

"Oh!" she exclaims, making sure Eureka has a good hold on the rope before letting go and momentarily disappearing.

The sunlight is just beginning to break across the sky. Morning has come. And I am being lowered into another dense darkness.

She returns with three white roses.

She gently weaves them into my hair amongst the forget-me-knots and dandelions.

I reach up to take her hand.

"Thank you," I say.

We hold hands for a moment. She kisses the top of my head and I see her wipe a tear from her eye.

She releases my hand and whistles again, this time not as loud.

Eureka begins to lower me into the well.

I hold onto the rope and reach up to touch the flowers in my hair.

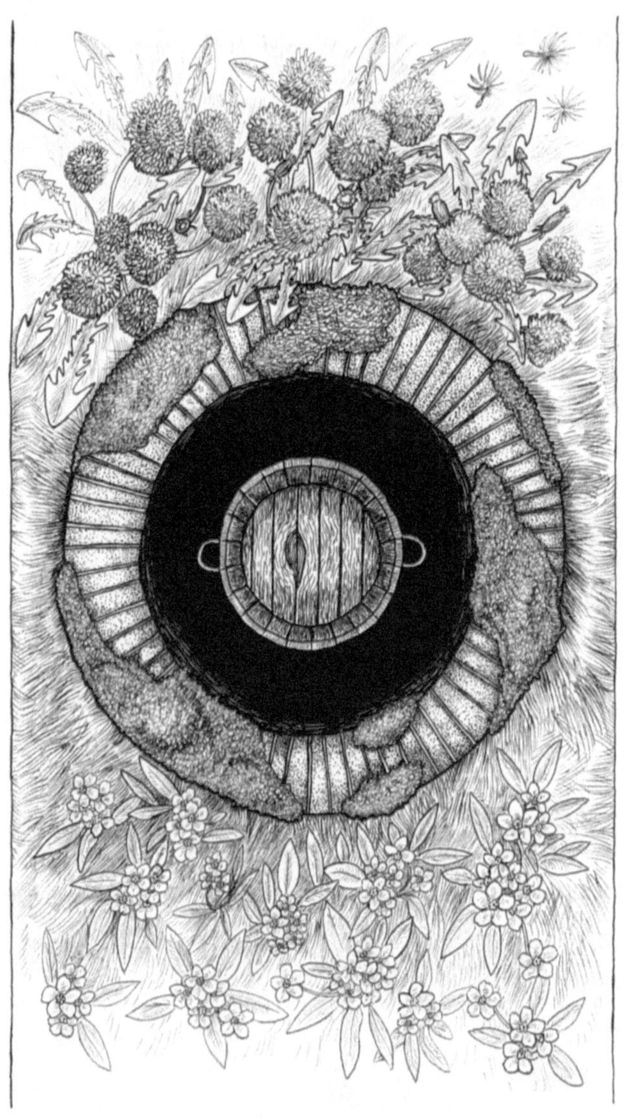

THE MIDDLE

It's Just a Song

A melody.
I can feel it whisper
To the strings of my heart.

Holding my hands,
It leads me onward slow,
Telling secrets only I know.

Past the first verse,
Intensity building
With every measure.

A memory,
Awakened, emboldened,
My eyelashes wet.

I am the notes
And they are me.
Cadence, familiar steps.

Harmonies fill my lungs
And give me hope.
My mind is finally quiet.

Compendium of sounds.
How does it elicit
A heartbeat so specific?

A Child at Play

There's a marble statue in the garden
Making crafts on the table, the bucket of beads overflows.
One got away and bounced off the patio,
click,

click,

click,

silence as it lands in the grass
The mesh plastic canvas paints
a chessboard, players made of yarn and
fresh cut cantaloupe and the smell of bacon
overtakes the flowers. Each piece of meat adds to
my waistline. Curved, textured, and cold like the statue
in the garden. With a freezer-burned fudgesicle in her hand.

Movement

I have an apple
On my desk
It sits

> I sit at my desk
> The apple
> Is still

The apple, it rolls
I jump up
And yell

> I didn't touch it
> It just moved
> By itself

I stare at my snack
On my desk
It sits

> I sit at my desk
> The apple
> Is still

My Appetite Is

Never satisfied.
I am hungry
for fortune
cookies
and something
fried. Say cheese
for the camera
that only adds
ten pounds
Over and over
weight is
Just a number.
And I just want to eat
my emotions, and color
on menus with crayons.

As a Woman

You wonder why I'm quiet
But scold me when I'm loud.
You tell me to sing along
But disapprove of the crowd.
You say, "Dress like a lady."
But my shoulders aren't allowed.
You ask to hold my hand,
Your other hand over my mouth.
You convince me that I'm lying
Without making a sound.
You cannot understand,
Your privilege too profound.

As a White Cis Woman

I wonder why you're quiet
But scold you when you're loud.
I tell you to sing along
But disapprove of the crowd.
I say, "Dress like a lady."
But your shoulders aren't allowed.
I ask to hold your hand,
My other hand over your mouth.
I convince you that you're lying
Without making a sound.
I cannot understand,
My privilege too profound.

Inside Out

This is the only flight out for days
And it feels like we've been here for years.
We've been traveling for almost seven
But only been in the airport for a couple.
Years and hours, respectively.
I have so many bags.
I'm always a little self-conscious
About the number of bags I travel with.
My travel companion has but one.
"How do you travel so light?" I ask.
He shrugs and we continue onward
Looking for our terminal.
Sometimes, he'll ask if I want his help.
I give him one of the heavy ones
And then sling three onto each arm.
They bump the large pack on my back,
Jostling the bag stacked on top of it.
I stand still for a moment and it settles.
I carefully squat to pick up the two remaining bags.
He looks on, trying to wait patiently.
He picks up the bag I set in front of him
And grimaces at the weight.
I apologize but he raises his hand to silence me.
"It's okay," he says. "But why do you still have all this?"
I hesitate. He's asked me this before
And he didn't like the answer.
"I don't really have a choice," I say.
He turns away so I can't see him roll his eyes.

When we first started traveling,
He'd gladly take half.
I'd offer to carry half of his luggage too.
Or even mix it in with mine.
But he refused every time.
We'd make our way through airports easily,
We'd run from plane to plane,
Soaring higher and higher,
Never looking down.
It was beautiful.
We were so young.
I still remember the first time
He opened one of my bags.
I think he was looking for toothpaste.
But it was the wrong bag
And he closed it quickly.
We didn't talk about it for a couple of weeks.
But finally, I asked him what he felt.
He tried to understand why I pack the way I do.
Once, he tried to tell me how to pack lighter.
I picked up his bag and asked him
To show instead of tell.
But he refused.
Every trip from then on,
I'd show him how I packed.
I told him how I worried
That I wouldn't have enough
Sweaters to keep me warm.
I think it was then

That he stopped carrying the bags.
He wanted to keep me warm.
And he tries to help me when he can.
His bag is heavier sometimes
And lighter others.
I've never looked inside.
"Here it is," he says.
Terminal twenty-two.
"Be careful," I say,
Wincing as he set my bag down with a thud.
He turns away to roll his eyes again.
"Turning away doesn't help.
I know you're rolling your eyes,"
I say, keeping my voice quiet.
His silence is loud.
"Let's talk about it," I say.
"Why do you still have all this stuff?"
"It's part of me," I say.
"It doesn't have to be."
"But I want it to be," I say.
He glances at his bag.

Lightning

The electricity
Coursing up my spine
Threatening
To sprout wings
From my scapula
Feathers jutting
From my back
And down my arms
So I can fly
Up to the lightning
To the unbearable
Bright, scorching white
Feeling dripping
From my fingers
Like blood
Emotion bubbling
In my stomach
Like acid
Dirt under my fingernails
Grounding me
Into dust

Them

Something in the way they hold their tea,
the way they smile easily.
Something in the way they hold their shoulders,
the way they grow bolder.
Something in the way they spoke my name,
the way they didn't lay claim.
Something in the way their mouth said please,
the way my mouth agreed.
Something in the way we moved together.
Something.

I Was Watching a Lot of Pride and Prejudice

Oh, but how my soured heart aches for the lies that seep from your lips. Enraptured at the mere memory of the sweet nothings floating away on the wind. How often must I find myself in the familiar throes of disdain? I yearn to build a home amongst the rocks. I know the tide will come in and I will drown but the white picket fence might hold. I darn the hole in my knitting as the water rises past the flowers in the garden, petals swaying in the current. I sip my tea as the waves crash through the windowpanes.

The fireplace doused,
the frigid water up to my knees,
I reach for the blanket I made for you
the night we fell in love.

All Sorts of Romance

Push my hair behind my ear
Like you're pulling back the curtains to let in the light.
Cradle my face
Like the horizon cradles the evening sun.
Put your hand on my back
Like we're walking through a crowd.
Pull me close
Like we're dancing
Like we've always been dancing.
Look into my eyes
Like you're looking through a telescope.
Tell me what you see
Tell me of my constellations.

Speak When You're Not Spoken To

I was quiet once
But only for a second
And now I'm loud
Enough to make up
For the silence

      I was lost and hell
      I'll always be
      Unless I continue
      To make the time
      Machine and go back
      To before sliced bread
      And coke bottle hips

            When time was slow
            The summer was hot
            And sweat slid down
            The back of my knees

Mother Mary

She rocks the baby, terrified.
Muscles stiff, she softly cries.
Not a single moment of clarity.
"This is not what it ought to be."

At the greatest depth of emotion,
Sad and afraid of the commotion.
He takes her hand, assuredly,
Though his eyes do not agree.

They gently examine this tiny face.
Search as she might for a trace
Of grace, she sees only a babe.
Brief, fleeting: a thought of escape.

A baby alone is a fearsome thing.
But what will this little angel bring?
Night waning, the moon defiant.
The baby's coos break the silence.

Her arms crossed, nestled between
She finds her son, an unfolding scene.
He opens his eyes, she comes undone.
Into her fabric, her soul, he is spun.

Regardless of the rest, all she knows
Is this sense welling within her bones.
It moves her to a trust far above all else.
She trusts this hope, this love, and herself.

The Book Was Me

I read / my Bible
went to the altar
to extinguish my candles
but they wouldn't go out.
I read / my Bible
ran to the pastor,
so furious, my verse
wasn't memorized.
I read / my Bible
Sang in the choir.
My voice was too loud.
The stained glass
Window broke.

Don't Mix Drinks

My thirty-three vertebrae
Chatter like teeth.
Stained glass windows cast
A patchwork quilt of colors
Across my hands and feet,
But pungent lilies are nothing
To secondhand smoke.

My heart rate rises
With the goosebumps
On my forearms.
Sticky floors remind me
Of sticky lips and handprints
On bathroom mirrors.

What if the chemical taste
Of bottom shelf spiced rum
Is my favorite perfume?

Still wanting clavicles and skin
And fingers roaming my hips,
I swallow shame
Like communion wine.
Open my jaw to sing a hymn.

Out soar black witch moths,
Wings painted with portraits
Of my face stained

With makeup and tears,
Finally freed from the place
They were planted.

Wild soaring creatures
Take hold of my hair
And lift me from my seat.
We crash through stained glass.
Shards of rainbow shower
My family and friends.

As we fly away,
The clouds closing in,
I thank my vast shame
For saving me once again.

Part III

The Rooms

As Eureka lowers me into the well, the old woman's dark silhouette lingers.

She's humming a vaguely familiar tune.

It echoes down to me like a penny dropped into one of those spiral wishing wells.

I look down to find I'm about halfway to the glowing hole in the wall.

As I get closer, the hole grows bigger.

Barely softer than the sound of the old woman's echoing hum, I hear something from the bottom of the well.

Out of the darkness comes the sounds of water, like the ripple of a buoy bobbing up and down in the moonlight. Or small waves slipping through the slats of a dock.

I train my eyes on every shadow, every shadow within a shadow, every piece of fine dust pushed over the edge of the well by the rope, stretching downward like fishing line.

As I approach the hole, I bend as much as I can to see into the opening.

Balancing like a failed rope dancer, I hang back.

A loud splash erupts from beneath me.

Something hurries out of the water like a bird taking flight.

I pull back to the rope as fast as I can, covering my head, preparing for a cloud of bats or something worse.

Nothing happens and the well is quiet again.

I open my eyes, to find the hole is directly in front of me. The edges are rough like the old stones had crumbled away over time. Remnants sit along the edges. Some seem to have been there for years. Others look like they could have fallen as I descended. Maybe that was the splash.

Finally able to look through the hole, I see a tunnel carved into the earth.

I yell up, "Stop, I'm here!"

"What do you see?" asks the old woman.

"There's a tunnel," I reply.

She says nothing.

I push off one side of the wall to swing myself into the opening. I land inside without much trouble.

Once again on solid ground, I peer up toward the old woman and Eureka but am greeted by only darkness.

"Hello?"

There is no response. The rope and bucket fall past the opening and splash into the water below. My stomach somersaults. My hands on the edge of the stone, I stare down into the abyss that is the rest of the well.

I try to remind myself that this is just a garden well and there's nothing scary waiting for me in the shadows. What solace I find dissipates when I turn around and remember I'm in a tunnel, carved in stone and earth, deep in the ground. A tunnel that just so happens to run into the side of a well in a garden in the woods where I took a walk two or three days ago.

My knees give way and I crumble to the ground.

The floor of the tunnel is cold and muddy. The water soaks through the knees of my jeans.

I lean forward into a lazy Child's Pose, putting my forehead against the cool surface.

I breathe deep and the smell of the wet stone fills my lungs.

It reminds me of creek walking when I was a child. Holding my mom's hand.

Time to go, I hear somewhere deep inside me.

I get up and wipe my forehead with my sleeve.

Every ten feet or so, small torches line the wall, set in metal holders.

The fire dances in a light breeze.

The tunnel slopes downward the further I go.

The walls are getting taller and I can see geological striations in the rock. I follow them with my fingers like I'm tracing grout lines.

The deeper into the tunnel that I walk, the more small plant life fossils pepper the walls.

I've been walking for quite some time and there's still no end in sight.

My pace increases. The cadence of my steps is almost foreign to me, born of some unconscious anxiety.

I break into a run.

The tunnel goes on and on.

And I run and run and run

Until I can't anymore.

I lean against the wall. My chest hurts, my lungs hurt, and I can feel my pulse ricocheting inside my skull.

I think I hear a whisper but it turns into a gust. The wind rushes down the tunnel and a few of the torches closest to me go out.

The tunnel is quiet until

Impish, breathy, elongated words ring in my ears.

"Get out," I hear, echoing down the tunnel. I can't tell which direction it's coming from.

Another gust of wind.

This one extinguishes all but a few of the torches.

Ice shoots through my veins as I hear a giggle.

It bounces from wall to wall.

I hear the raspy, ragged breath before I feel it on my cheek.

My gut is telling me to keep going.

I take two and a half steps before I'm stopped in my tracks.

Even in the low light, I can clearly see there is nothing in front of me, but I feel the hands on my shoulders. With one solid shove, they push me backward.

The force knocks me over and I fall hard on my back, my head hitting the floor.

I get up as quickly as I fell.

I shake the dizziness from my eyes and the pain from my head.

I look around for whatever might come but nothing does.

I keep doing this ridiculous defensive dance until my heart rate begins to slow.

Step by slow, methodical step, I make my way forward, past the last of the torches.

Exhaustion rolls over me, settling in my head.

Through a thick brain fog, I see a wall ahead of me.

Does the tunnel just end? Is this it?

My eyes begin to adjust and I realize the tunnel takes a sharp right. Around the corner, I'm greeted by a large archway. Past the archway, a large room.

I feel a little like a fish about to swim from the reef and into open water.

I know I should keep going. I want to keep going. I'm just scared. Being scared is okay. It's doesn't mean I don't keep going.

I step into the room.

Nothing happens.

I take another step before my toe catches on something and I almost trip.

I look down to see that the ground looks different here.

I'm no longer standing on stone but something wooden.

Searching with my hands to compensate for what my vision lacks in the poor light, I finally find what I tripped on.

A doorknob?

A small metal doorknob sticking up from the wooden paneled door in the ground under my feet.

Realizing I'm standing on top of a door gives me a sudden rush of vertigo and I hurry to the solid ground to the left of the door.

I kick something else that skitters around on the ground. Something metal again and from the sound, it twirls in place like a New Year's Eve spinning noisemaker.

I bend to examine it closer and eventually find a bolt in the floor next to the door with a key on it.

I finagle a metal skeleton key from the bolt and hold it up in hopes I'll be able to see it better. I can't.

I wipe my sweaty hands on my jacket and notice there's something in my pocket. It's cool to the touch, something round, almost like a ring. There's a small cylinder connected to the ring with a wheel at the top.

The finger flasher magic trick.

When had she put it in my pocket?

I take it out and put it on my finger. I spin the wheel to ignite the ring but nothing happens.

The flash cotton.

I check my other pocket and find a small round cotton-ball-size piece of fluff. Enough for maybe four or five small explosions.

Well, I think, *it's better than nothing.*

I kneel to try the key in the door on the ground. It doesn't turn. I try the handle anyway. It doesn't open.

I put the key in my pocket and gaze out into the darkness.

I blink hard.

Did I really see something?

A small white line directly in front of me.

It's so small that if I stare at it too hard, it seems to disappear.

It reminds me of laying on the dock along the river at midnight. It was always darker at the river.

We were always there for the Perseid meteor shower. We would lay out night after night, staring up into the cosmos. Between the shooting stars, we'd pick our quadrants and look for a star to befriend. Each time, I'd stare too long at one and it would disappear. I found the phenomenon so interesting I'd sometimes miss a beautiful cascade of rock burning up in our atmosphere instead of a tiny star playing hide and seek.

There was always a chill in the air.

I shiver.

The small line of light draws me in like a bug zapper.

I walk slowly, gingerly so as not to fall down some unseen staircase or a large hole lying in wait.

As I draw near, I see the light is coming from beneath another door. This one is on the wall where it belongs.

Each careful step brings me closer until I finally make contact with the opposite wall.

I feel like I've overcome some great test even though all I've really done is walk across a room in the dark.

From what I can tell, it's just like the door on the floor outside the corridor.

This means there's probably a —

Key.

Here it is, on a bolt.

This time, the key turns and I hear two distinct clicks.

Even the patchy light of the room beyond makes me squint.

Two blue couches frame a living room with two rectangular windows high on the wall.

Two golden rectangles paint the familiar brown carpet as the afternoon sun pours in.

One sits directly in front of a staircase leading to the second floor and my attic bedroom.

A finished attic with slanted ceilings creating two cubbies on each end of the room.

It made me feel like a princess.

I gaze through the door and my childhood home stares back at me.

A gust of wind rushes past me and through the door as if trying to push me into the house.

Into the past.

The house is quiet and the dust rustled by the breeze dances on the rays of sunlight. The high windows were the perfect height to welcome the afternoon beams, streaking from one side of the room to the other.

I step into the room and suddenly, the doorknob is next to my ear.

I haven't fallen but still reach for the handle to steady myself.

My hands are so small. I look down and my whole body is small.

I'm wearing one of my favorite pair of floral pants and a striped shirt. I'd picked my own clothes.

I step back into the large room and watch myself transform.

I watch as my bones expand and my skin begins to age. My tattoo reappears on my arm. It happens so quickly that I barely have time to take it in.

"Echo?"

It's coming from the doorway. Inside the house.

"Are you out there?" says a woman's voice.

The sound of my mom's voice in this moment is too much for me to stand. My shoulders bow forward, my abdomen contracts, and my face contorts into an emotional display of everything I've encountered over the last few days on this —whatever this is.

A sob heaves from my throat and echoes into the darkness.

"I hear you, but I can't see you," my mom continues.

I think about racing around the door frame and collapsing into her arms but something in my gut tells me not to. Something isn't right.

"Sweet girl, come back to safety. I'm here. We're here," she says.

"We're all here, Echo," I hear my brother's voice.

"We're waiting for you to come home," says my dad's voice.

It's too much.

I race around the door and watch as my outstretched arms shrink to my five-year-old body once again. My mom, dad, and brother get down to their knees as I approach and they envelop me in a hug. I feel like I could disappear in it. In fact, I know I could. I can feel how happy they are to have me home like a force, pressing down on my skin.

My dad speaks first. "I'm so glad you're back where you belong."

My mom is next. "It'll be different, you'll see."

Then my brother. "We'll grow together this time."

The pressure of their hug increases as if they're trying to make me smaller.

I'm already so much smaller.

Then I see it. I realize.

This isn't deeper in,

This is an off-ramp.

I could stay here. It wants me to stay here.

But this isn't my family.

I'm not a child anymore.

I try to break free of their hug but they do not release me.

It's like they have more arms than three humans should.

"You belong here," says my dad.

"You're our baby," says my mom.

"You're my little sister," says my brother.

I struggle against their arms.

"You don't belong anywhere else," says my dad.

"You have to be my little good girl," says my mom.

"We're just trying to love you," says my brother.

I push and pull but my small arms are not very strong.

"Let me go," I squeak out.

"How can you ask us to do that?" asks my dad.

"Don't you love us?" asks my mom.

"Why are you struggling?" asks my brother.

"I'm not five anymore. I'm thirty," I say. Listening to my tiny voice say these words, even I don't believe them.

My mom and dad laugh but my brother is silent.

"You're so funny," says my mom. She and my dad laugh some more.

My brother is still silent.

"I don't want to be here. I need to go home," I say, beginning to panic.

"You are home," says my dad.

My brother finally speaks, "You are sick. Mom and dad can laugh but I know the truth. You need help. You're confused. Let me help you."

I make eye contact with him, wondering what this means.

He begins to push the arms away from me.

I'm so surprised, that I don't immediately run.

He puts his hands on my shoulders.

"You're my little sister. You need to be careful what you say or people might think you're crazy."

I gaze into his eyes for what my gut tells me is longer than I should.

I'm looking for something.

The thing I've seen so many times before.

But his eyes are hollow.

"This isn't real," I say. My voice sounds more like myself now.

I back away from him and his arms fall back to his side.

I look into my parents' eyes the way I looked into my brother's.

"None of you are real," I say.

I step back out the door and into the large room.

They still kneel in a semi-circle just inside the door but they now meet my thirty-year-old eyes.

"If you close that door, you can never come back," says my dad. His eyes swell.

"If you close that door, I don't know what I can do to help you," says my mom. Her voice breaks.

"If you close that door," my brother starts. His face is solemn, "You'll lose yourself."

One after the other, I meet each of their eyes to make sure. It's not there. Love. Their immovable, unconditional love is not there.

Realization washes over me and I feel my heart brighten.

I step back into the room just enough to grab the doorknob.

I don't shapeshift this time but the creatures before me do.

They lunge forward.

I pull the door shut.

I expect them to bang on the door but all I hear are soft thumps and a low scratching noise near the base.

I hold the doorknob as tight as I can and rummage in my pocket for the key.

The click of the lock shifting into place is a sweet sound.

I hear another click.

I back away from the door.

But the door doesn't move.

More clicks. Faster now. As if something mechanical is revving up.

I'm jolted forward against the door as the floor begins to move.

In the dark, it's hard to process what is happening but I hear what sounds like stone grinding against stone.

Vertigo is kicking in. I close my eyes and swallow hard like I'm stuck on some terrible carnival ride trying not to puke.

The whole room feels like it's rotating.

I hear another series of clicks. The grinding slows and then stops.

I open my eyes to find myself now lying on the door that led to my childhood home. The door is on the floor just like the first one.

I look out into the darkness and sure enough, a small line of light reaches me from across the room.

Slowly, gingerly, I walk to the door and go directly for the key.

I shove it into the keyhole, trying to ignore my constant state of exhaustion laced with fear.

This is the next thing. The room behind this door.

I push it open and it bangs against a desk.

The room is bright and white.

The air smells sterile and clean with a lingering sweetness.

Through the door lies a laboratory.

A wall is lined with tanks, holding what looks like human forms. The glass is curved, distorting the view.

I take a step into the room.

I don't transform this time.

I hear something that sounds like a shower curtain being pulled from one end of the metal rod to the other.

The metal-on-metal screech makes my neck muscles tense.

A person emerges from a hallway at the back of the room.

They are covered from head to toe in plastic. A long white loose-fitting gown with plastic pants and boots beneath. The hood is up over their head, secured with a mask. The mask is transparent at the eyes but covers the rest of their face. Their large white gloves go up past their elbows. They crinkle as they walk.

"Good, you're here," they say, their voice slightly muffled.

I stay quiet.

"Did you bring your donor paperwork?" they ask.

"Paperwork?" I ask.

They walk to the desk behind the door and pull out a clipboard. They examine it carefully before taking a few notes and looking back at me.

"You're here because of the accident, right?" they ask.

"What accident?" I ask.

They sigh.

"The bus? You have some connection to these people," they say, flipping a page on the clipboard and handing it to me.

I take the clipboard.

I read through the list on the page and feel a palpitation press against my chest from the inside. Just one.

I hold in my hands a comprehensive list of my best friends.

The sheet is broken into columns. The first contains their names, the second cites their injury, the third has handwritten notes about how serious the injuries are, and the fourth column notates what organ replacements are required. The fifth and final column stated whether the person was alive or "in stasis".

"What happened to them?" I ask, trying to remember that this isn't real.

"You did," the technician says.

They try to take the chart back, but I pull it away and flip to the front page.

I had been driving us all to a party and had flipped the bus.

I was the only one who walked away without injury.

The technician grabs the clipboard back, showing some annoyance.

"You decided to donate organs to help," they say. "Ya know since this was your fault."

I'm quiet again.

"You didn't change your mind, did you?" they ask.

"No," I blurt out.

Jesus Christ, Echo. Really? This isn't even real.

"Good," they say, eyeing me like I might run out the door again.

"What am I donating?" I ask.

They laugh. "You saw the list. What AREN'T you donating?"

"I obviously can't donate all that," I say.

The technician looks at me for a long minute. It seemed like she was trying to figure out if I was serious or not. They rummage through the paper on the clipboard before handing it back to me.

"Well, there's your signature," they say.

I look at the signature, sure it won't match.

But it does.

It's then that I look at the wall next to us. I can now see into the first chamber clearly and there, I see her, eyes closed and floating in a blueish-green liquid.

I walk toward her and put my hand on the glass.

It's freezing to the touch.

This face that I've seen smile, laugh, cry, and all the emotions between, is lifeless.

My body doubles over and I feel my heart and stomach making their way up to my throat. The feeling continues upward until the contents of my stomach are on the floor in front of me.

The technician runs out of the room, I assume to get someone or something to clean up the mess I made.

I'm still doubled over.

I shouldn't have opened this door. I shouldn't have stepped in.

I peer back into the chamber.

Her hair floats around her face like I've seen it blow in the wind so many times.

I look down the row and run to the next.

And the next.

Each holds one of my beloveds. Those that I know will always carry my heart and I theirs. But there are only three in this room.

The technician returns shortly with cleaning supplies.

"Where are the rest?" I ask.

They sigh again.

"Where are they?" I can't keep my voice from getting louder.

"Are you going to puke on them too?" they ask.

I take a step toward them, not sure what I'd do next.

The technician scoffs, "They're down the hall. Don't make a mess."

I look toward the hall and then back at the door to the large room. It's still open.

"Leave that open," I point at the door as I make my way down the hall.

The first room I come to has the curtain drawn.

I grab the chart from the basket on the wall outside the room and read it quickly.

I slowly walk toward the curtain and pull it back just enough to see inside.

She'd been sleeping but at the soft jingle of the metal rings on the curtain rod, she stirs.

"Echo?" she asks.

I run to her side and hold her hand, "I'm here."

"They said you died in the crash," she says.

My brow furrows but I reply, "No, no, I'm fine. I'm here. I'm going to help."

She opens her eyes wider. I'm not sure whether I should get a nurse until I hear the soft gurgle of a chuckle seep from her mouth. "Don't be ridiculous. A rod punctured a valve on my heart. You can't just give me your heart."

"I already signed the papers," I say.

She slowly lifts her hand to my face, "I love you, but you're an idiot. Echo," she says, grabbing the collar of my shirt and pulling me closer. "This isn't real. I know it feels real when you're looking at me lying here but it's not real. You need to know that. You have to know that."

"But you're dying. All of you. And it's my fault," I say, a few tears dripping from my chin onto the white blanket.

"But we're not, Echo. You are. You're dying," she says. "This is all a dream. I know it's hard to separate when you see us hurting right in front of you. Everyone is hurting. But we're all adults."

Her voice lowers to a whisper, "You're the only one trying to sign away your life to save someone who doesn't need saving."

"But you need me!" I say, gesturing to her in the bed.

"I do need you, you're right. I need you to be alive," she says. "Now go. Hurry."

The technician pulls the curtain back, breaking my concentration.

This time, the metal scraping of the curtain sounds more like an echo from a memory.

I catch a waft of lavender in the air.

I look from the technician to my friend. She's still in the hospital bed but doesn't look sick anymore.

She mouths the word, "Run."

I run as fast as I can back down the hall.

As I round the corner back into the room with the chambers, another technician, or the same technician, I can't tell, is closing the door to the stone room.

"No," I yell, but they're already locking it.

I pull the technician away from the door as hard as I can sending them sliding across the floor.

I fish the key from my pocket and my adrenaline-filled hands have trouble getting the key into the keyhole. I hear the grinding of stone from outside the door. The outside room is already turning.

Finally, I hear the double click of the lock and pull the door open.

The moment the door opens, the laboratory floor shifts to match the incline of the large room outside. The large room had already turned enough that the sudden rotation throws the technician backward just before they can grab me.

I throw my arms ahead of me and take hold of the doorframe, pulling myself up and out of the door. Reaching back in to pull the door closed, I see the technician standing on the back wall, looking for a way to climb up the slick floor they had just cleaned.

I pull the door closed and lock it, leaning back on the wall that will soon be the floor and listen to the grinding stone.

The stone grinds to a stop as the room finishes another quarter rotation.

The wall is now the floor yet again and the door to the lab upon it.

I scramble to my feet.

Without having to look for it, I see the next thin white light blink into existence across the room.

This one is brighter.

Its pull is greater.

I open the door and sunbeams shine directly onto my face.

My house is quiet except for morning sounds. The coffee pot percolating, sleepy feet shuffling. I hear the back door open and close. The dog shakes and her collar jingles.

My husband walks around the corner toward the front door. Probably on his way to his office in the front of the house.

"Back from your walk?" he says.

I look behind me and still see the large room looming over me.

He continues past me and my befuddled face.

The calm of my environment only makes my heart beat faster and my stomach churn harder.

Leaving the door open, I follow him.

By the time I reach the office, he's already sitting behind his desk.

He raises his eyes to meet mine.

"Are you okay?" he asks.

My vision gets spotty and I lean against the wall to stabilize myself.

"What's going on?" he asks, still behind his desk.

"I —I'm not —," I begin, but I can't finish my thought.

I back out of the room, feeling beads of sweat on my forehead.

My dog meets me in the hallway with a wag of her tail.

I see the open front door, the darkness of the large room seeps in, casting a shadow like the opposite of a sunbeam.

"Echo?" I hear my husband say from behind me.

My head is doing the doggie paddle in ten-foot waves. I can't seem to get a full breath before I'm forced back under.

The doorknob is suddenly the same height as my ear again but this time, I've fallen to my knees.

Am I home? I think.

It's the last thing I remember before waking up on the couch in our living room.

Some Twitch streamer is on the television. My husband is sitting on the ground in front of the couch staring at my face.

"Are you ok?" he asks again.

I try to take stock before answering. My head hurts, my stomach still feels like it's being dropped off a high building every few minutes, I'm covered in sweat, and my vision is still fading in and out.

"I think I'm okay," I say.

"Too long a walk?" he asks.

"Maybe," I respond.

"You passed out," he says.

"I don't remember how I got home," I say without much thought behind it.

He pauses but then says, "Well, you're home now."

"How long was I out?" I ask.

"Only a few seconds, really. You kind of melted by the door and then came to enough for me to help you to the couch," he says.

"I had some really strange hallucinations," I say.

"In those few seconds?" he asks.

"Yeah, I guess," I say.

The door.

Something about the door.

I feel it in my gut.

"You, uh, you look pretty rough for just going on a walk in the woods," he says, chuckling.

I reach up and touch the flowers in my hair.

"I like your crown," he says.

I smile and push myself up off the couch, "Thanks."

My whole body aches.

"I feel like I got hit by a truck."

"You look like you got hit by a truck," he says with a sly smile on his face.

"Yeah, yeah, yeah. Thanks. I think I'm gonna shower," I say.

"Okay," he says.

I stand up slowly, testing the water of balance.

I'm steadier than I thought I'd be.

I head to the bedroom, passing the foyer.

Something pulls me toward the door.

The foyer is still lit with morning light. My jacket hangs on a hook next to the door. He must have hung it up after I fainted.

I place my hand on the door before opening it.

"What're you doing now, weirdo?" my husband asks.

"I —I don't know," I say.

I open the door.

The welcome mat has the same old leaves tucked around it, the garden is green, and the neighborhood is waking up.

I close the door.

THE ON-GOING

"I Am From" Poem

I am from the yellow tattered baby blanket that still sits on my bed.
From Chiavetta's Marinade and Weber's Horseradish Mustard.
I am from the slanted ceiling attic bedroom, cozy and warm.
The unfinished wood covering the crawl space is rough to the touch,
My soft fingers begging for a sliver.
I am from lilac bushes and tiger lilies
Planted on the hill at the end of grandma's house,
The part of the garden no one tended.
I'm from homemade kielbasa and compassion.
From Ken and Becky.
I'm from pay-it-forward and prayer.
From I love you and you're so sensitive.
I'm from the Lutheran Missouri Synod, my confirmation verse
"Now faith is being sure of what you hope for and certain of what you do
not see."
I'm from Buffalo and the Reeds.
Fresh caught, hand fileted Northern Pike and pretzels.
From the dirndls and lederhosen we wore when my dad and Russ carried
me through the Oktoberfest on a beer barrel, a rite of passage.
From the troll under the pool deck that brought my brother slurpies and
nachos.
I have replicated a hallway in my parent's house.
Theirs filled floor to ceiling with family photos, plaques, awards, childhood
drawings, and pictures of Jesus.
Mine filled with photos of family by blood and family by love.
Both hallways remind me what I am made of and what I try to be.
They remind me of how inherently part of my family I am
And what it means to feel loved.

Roots and Blooms

When you're a child
Sometimes all you know
Is how to be someone's shadow.

You don't know where they'll lead
Or what you might find
But when you look up,
You see their smile against the sky.

When you're a child
You never keep track
You might not even consider having to look back.

And one day, you may look down
And find something you've lost.
See you've fallen behind, appalled at the cost.
But then, something happens.
Something magic, you see.
You realize you're now your own.
You've been set free.

Oh, little girl blues,
Stay where you are.
The sun is warm and bright,
The night full of stars.

Clean

Today in the bath, I counted
The moles on my legs,
Traced my incisions,
And charted my stretch marks
Like a constellation.
The hum of the fan
Harmonizing
With the water
Somehow still leaking
Down the plugged drain.
I pressed on the plug with my heel.

The window in the bathroom, open
Blinds, just enough to see the sky.
The knockdown textured wall
Displayed a gradient of color,
Bright by the window
And dark further in.
There was a scuff mark
Under the counter
That I'd never seen before.
My tattoos looked beautiful
Under the purple water.

The warmth of the water, me,
Cool steel, enameled porcelain,
Pear and Honey.
My fingers had pruned,
Callouses had softened.
I watched the water
Rush down the drain,
A small whirlpool formed,
My favorite part:
When I felt more than saw
Something circle and disappear.

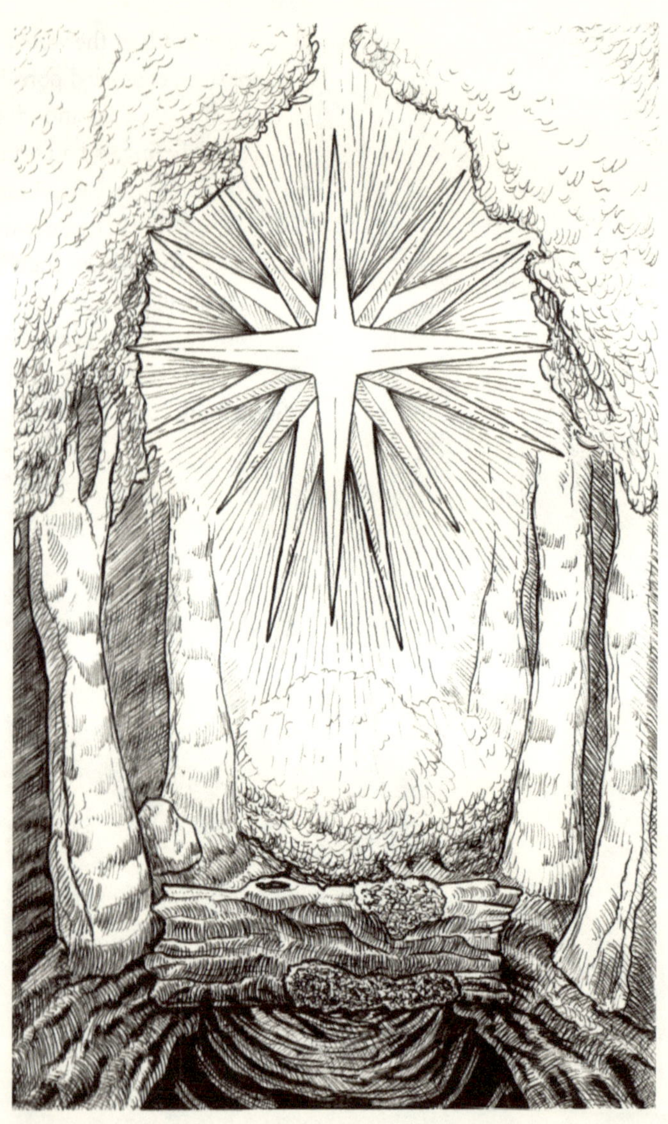

Sacred Ground

There is a place I always go,
The sunlight, warm and bright.
The road is dangerous, I know.
The railroad tracks in sight.
Ev'ry third time, I'd pass it by,
The entrance, hard to see.
I'd never find it when I'd try.
I had to let my mind fly free.
Then through the thicket, through I go,
Each step a cherished rite
The branches stretched upward just so,
Spilling patches of light.
A roof of green breaks up the sky,
The ground covered in leaves.
I leave reality behind
And walk across the fallen tree.

My portal to a secret world
Where everything is clear.
Where my sails are free to unfurl
And heartbeats whisper in my ear.

I walk across the fallen tree
And leave reality behind.
The ground covered in leaves,
A roof of green breaks up the sky.
Spilling patches of light,
The branches stretched upward just so.
Each step a cherished rite.
Through the thicket, through I go.
I had to let my mind fly free,
I'd never find it if I'd try.
The entrance, hard to see.
Ev'ry third time, I'd pass it by.
The railroad tracks in site,
The road, dangerous, I know.
But the sunlight is warm and bright.
In the place I always go.

Fish Tale

I had somehow forgotten that I was a sailor.
Forgotten how, the story, I chose to tailor.

The memories ebb and flow like the briny waves.
Exhuming my heart and soul from freshly dug graves.

The ship, she ran like a golden machine.
My apple, my rite, my Fiddler's Green.

Monstro swimming circles 'round my head,
Davy Jones shakes my hand, tells me I'm not dead.

Pirates maraud amidst my piles of stones.
Flesh becomes aware of skull and crossbones.

That's when I realize, when I understand and
I run from stern to bow, my sword in my hand!

Greeted by my angelic figurehead friend,
I look down at the water, my sword I extend.

And I promise, right there, to be honest and true.
To never lose sight of the sailor I knew.

The sailor I am, more water to explore.
Setting sail to sail, not for the opposite shore.

Whether a love, a whale, the bay, the sea.
I had forgotten. The one that got away
Was me.

Bedtime Poem

Pajamas on, she gets in bed.
Moving pillows, avoiding dread.
She turns off the light and into the night,
Blankets, sheets, over her head.

She does not see but only feels
A presence that is all too real.
Face it, she must. In herself, she must trust.
She throws off her blankets with zeal.

The demon close, warming her skin,
It sees her soul, the pain within.
Gently it wraps her in a tender grasp.
She's scared but her fear wears thin.

Its warmth does not burn like the dead,
Instead, it warms like fresh-baked bread.
"I will hold thee as long as thou need me,"
It growls and sets her in bed.

Her guardian demon hugged her.
She fell asleep in its fur.
When she awoke like a fever that broke,
She welcomed what trouble could stir.

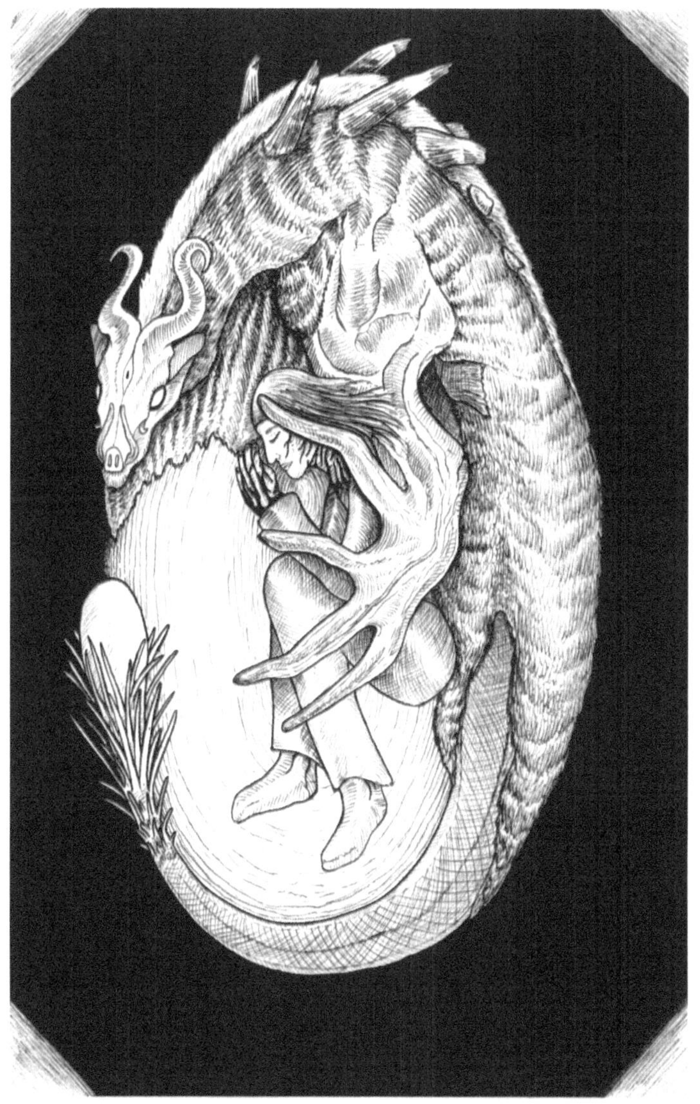

Lightbulbs

You are so bright, my dear.
You will blind some.
Others will want to bask in your glow.
But all will hold onto you
As if their lives depended on it.
If there's one thing our souls know when we're born,
It's that you never let go of the luminous.

Relationships Are Hard

I love the way we laugh.
But I also love diving into the depths
Of the tears I cry to see
How long I can hold my breath.
I love who I am when I'm with you.
I love her so much that sometimes,
I forget she's my imaginary friend.
I will always love you.
And you will always love me
The way I used to love myself.

Name

All my wants, wishes, and needs
Need not be part of you.
I only ask
That when you are strong,
You wear them.
Drape my wants around your shoulders
Like a royal mantle.
Set a crown of my wishes atop your head
And wield my needs like a great sword.
A sharp and studied sword.
A sword of mercy.
I will not fret
When your mantle is draped over the armchair,
Your crown is on the kitchen table,
And your great sword is sheathed.
You need not always be a king
And I will never ask you to bow
As I will never bow to you.
But you are only welcome here
If you know my name.

Easy

It would be so easy to surrender to "love".
All I would have to do is let go.
Let go of inhibitions and trauma.
Let go of the boundaries I've struggled to build, brick by brick.
Let go of the hard-won wisdom I'm proud to have gathered in this harsh weather.
I could set it all down and touch your hand.
And I know how good it would feel.
How my hand would flex after the pleasure of your skin.
Sometimes I am quiet and let the familiar turbulence wash over me.
Sometimes I even let it in.
But I cannot, will not linger there.
And I cherish the moment
I know it's time to leave.
It's a new feeling, a steady feeling,
The boat finally pushing against the sand
After surviving a great storm.
I love the sway of the sea but the smell of the earth has won my heart.
Yet just for a little while longer
I'll stand on the shore,
Look out over the waves,
And wish I had a bigger boat.

Part IV

The Mirror

Days pass.

My life is the same as it ever has been.

The first day after I fainted in the foyer, I slept all day.

I try to remember the walk I took in the woods and why I came home the way I did.

Cold, exhausted, dehydrated, confused.

I don't even remember the last time I actually passed out.

They say stress can do unbelievable things to the body and for the first time, I understand.

The stress flows in my veins like tiny carnivorous creatures, taking bites out of each organ they happen past.

My husband is unfazed by my concerns about that day. Save thinking his partner has gone a little bonkers.

We don't talk much about our feelings.

I think that was one of the reasons I had gone for that walk in the first place.

Even that feels like inventing a narrative rather than remembering one.

If not for the dreams, I'd probably have let that go by now too.

But the dreams.

To say they have been vivid is an understatement. They have been visceral.

I wake up covered in sweat, my side of the bed soaked through like I'd taken a shower and used the cocoon of my sheets to dry myself.

As I fall asleep each night, I hear scratching in the walls.

When the spinning ceiling fan manages to hum me to sleep, my dreams mimic the sound with low growls.

In the wakeful morning hours, I see shadows clinging to the corners of the room that pulse like breath being drawn in and pushed out.

The dreams are always the same.

I'm standing in my living room, in the middle of the house.

I am conscious and alive but my body is made out of wood. I'm only able to move certain joints in certain directions as if I was built with a purpose I'm not aware of. My edges are rough like I was thrown from the workshop early.

My dog lays at my feet and my husband goes about his day.

I watch.

I listen.

The first night I dreamt of the wooden woman, that was where the dream ended.

Each following night, it progressed.

I stood in the middle of the room like a statue and the world moved around me.

I wanted to move so badly but all I could do was bend my elbows, waist, and neck like the forgotten sister of a Truly Scrumptious music box.

The sheer torture of wanting to move.

One dream seemed to last a week. I remember crying in the dream, a drip of sap squeezing from between the grain of my eye.

Like a waking nightmare, sometimes merely thinking about the dream makes me enter the realm.

Each night, the same static, coarse existence.

Until tonight.

Tonight, my husband approaches the wooden woman, his hands behind his back.

"I'm going to help you," he says.

"Can you help me walk?" I ask.

"Just let me help," he says.

From behind his back, he brings an electric sander in one hand and safety goggles in the other. He meets my eye expecting gratitude.

I have to carve each new expression onto my face but do my best to smile.

The gritty buzz of the sander scares our dog and she runs to the bedroom.

Soon, the room smells of sawdust.

He starts with my right arm, sanding down the rough spots.

It feels a little like getting a pedicure at a spa where they use all the best callous removal techniques. I watch as my skin flies through the air, relaxing into the experience.

I watch as the lines of my forearm appear and the curves of my bicep take shape.

Sawdust dances around me in slow motion like confetti in celebration of the new woman I'll be.

My attention is drawn back to my arm as the sander goes beyond just smoothing my rough edges and removes more and more of my body.

It starts to burn.

"You need to stop," I say.

He can't hear me above the whir of the sander.

The pain increases —

Until I wake up with a scream of pain.

"Are you ok?" asks my groggy husband next to me in bed. "Another bad dream?"

I nod, my hand on my chest.

"You were talking again," he says, rolling over to look at me.

"What this time," I ask.

"Just kept saying 'you need to stop'," he says.

I don't say anything.

He rustles next to me. I don't realize what's happening until he's standing next to the bed, having clicked on the light on his nightstand, and yelling, "Echo!"

I look down at my arm to find brush burns covering the length of it, a deeper wound on my bicep. The sheets are covered with my sweat and blood.

"What the fuck?" he says.

I slowly get out of bed, holding my arm so as not to drip on the carpet.

"Do you need anything?" he asks.

"I'm just going to clean it out. Can you get the gauze?"

"Medicine cabinet?"

I examine my arm in the bathroom mirror but nod to him before continuing.

No sawdust. Just blood.

I clean the cuts and brush burns with gentle antibacterial soap and dry them with a washcloth. He returns with the gauze and I bandage my arm while he watches from the edge of the bed.

I stare at myself in the mirror for a moment.

There's something wrong with the mirror. It's looking back at me.

I shake it off and sigh.

I start back into the bedroom and am met with a look of sincere confusion from my husband.

"I don't know. Maybe I was walking in my sleep again," I say.

"I would have noticed," he says.

"You've been sleeping harder lately," I say.

We're both quiet for a long time. I finally make my way back to my side of the bed, forgetting the mess waiting for me.

"Wanna get new sheets?" I ask him.

He leaves the room and I begin to pull the sheets off the bed.

At the base of the bed, as I untuck the fitted sheet and wrap the top sheet in it, I feel a puncture on the tip of my finger like a pinprick.

I look at my finger to find the end of a small wooden sliver sticking out of my soft skin.

I start to feel dizzy again.

He returns with the sheets and sees me falter.

He drops the sheets and runs to me.

He helps me sit on the edge of the bed.

"You know you can talk to me, right?" he asks.

I look at his face.

I want his blue-grey eyes to see through me.

"Maybe in the morning," I say.

The dizzy spell passes.

But I don't sleep again.

The morning sun rises, stripes of light shining between the hanging blinds, turning the room into a bright painted jail cell. I can barely hear the blinds click-clack against each other, air pushed through them by our ceiling fan.

I don't think my husband slept either.

He's already out of bed and in the kitchen making coffee.

He brings me a cup and sets it on my nightstand.

He goes back to his side of the bed and sets his cup on his nightstand before getting back in bed, but sitting up this time.

"It's morning," he says.

I sigh deep enough that I feel the air reach the bottom of my lungs before pushing it back out.

"Thank you for the coffee," I say.

He turns to me, "I just want to be here for you."

"I know," I say. I meet his eyes and repeat myself, "I know. Really."

He looks back at his cup of coffee.

I sit up, propping a pillow behind me. I hold my cup of hot coffee like a raccoon holding the last piece of dumpster pizza on earth. It smells of hazelnut and cinnamon.

"Echo," he says, pointing at my arm.

I look at it, expecting to see the bandage bled through.

But there is no blood.

Even the brush burns are gone.

I set my coffee down and unwrap my arm where the deepest wound was. There is nothing but my skin beneath the bandage.

My husband is quiet.

I am quiet.

I don't understand.

"What is going on?" he whispers.

"I don't know," I respond.

"Things haven't been right since you got back from that walk," he says.

"I know," I say.

"Did you really just go to the woods?" he asks.

I search his face to determine his meaning but there's nothing more to read.

"As far as I know," I respond.

He sighs.

Then, like someone played the last note on a jack-in-the-box, he jumps out of bed.

He's gone from the room before I can even ask where he's going.

He returns with my jacket.

The one I'd worn on my walk.

He's has something in his hand.

"This stuff is still in your pockets from that day," he says.

He throws a small metal ring on the bed and a cotton ball.

He puts his hand into the other pocket and brings out four skeleton keys.

"What is this stuff?" he asks.

I shrug.

The keys all look similar but one is different than the rest. It has three grooves in the stem. They look about the size of the other three keys. Sure enough, the others slide into place, filling in some missing pieces of the bit.

But what is the key for?

My husband figures out how to use the metal ring, placing some cotton into a small cylinder and flicking what looks like the mechanism on a lighter. A small burst of flame appears over his hand.

"How did you do that?" I ask.

"My dad used to have one of these when I was a kid. It's a finger flasher. You put the cotton here and then flick this." He shows me.

I try it.

In that moment while the flames still hang in the air, I hear a voice.

"Did you hear that?" I ask him.

He stands stock-still and listens.

We listen.

"I don't hear anything," he says.

I load the finger flasher again and turn the small wheel.

The same warmth on my fingers, the same small explosion, and the same whisper from between the flames.

"The flames? I heard the little explosion thingie," says my husband.

"There was a voice," I say. "It said something 'isn't real'."

The door.

The door isn't real?

Now it's my turn to run from the room.

I throw the keys to my husband as I leave.

I make it to the foyer and approach the front door with caution.

I can see the light of day through the half-moon window above the door.

I open it.

Just in time to wave to the mailperson and watch my neighbor pull out of their driveway to get to work. They wave too.

"You really don't remember what these keys are for?" I jump at the sound of his voice. I didn't realize he'd followed me into the hall.

"Let me see them," I say, stretching one hand toward him, closing the door with the other.

When the keys meet my finger, all the blood drains from my head like I stood up too quick. It's replaced by a rush of memories. The days I spent in the woods, in the garden, in the tunnel, in the rooms.

I remember it all as I hear the front door latch behind me.

I back away from the door slowly.

I look at my husband.

His first instinct is to run toward the door to see what I must have seen outside.

"Don't open it," I say.

He continues toward it.

"Don't!" I yell.

He stops and turns to look at me.

"I remember everything," I say.

We move to the couch without speaking.

We sit and he waits.

"You're going to think I'm crazy."

"Too late for that," he says with half a smirk, trying to make light and make me smile.

"You're not going to like what I have to tell you," I continue. The remaining smirk leaves his face. "I went on the walk that day to think. To think about everything."

I tell him about every step I took, every choice I made, every person and thing I met along the way. I told him about the enormous room that awaits

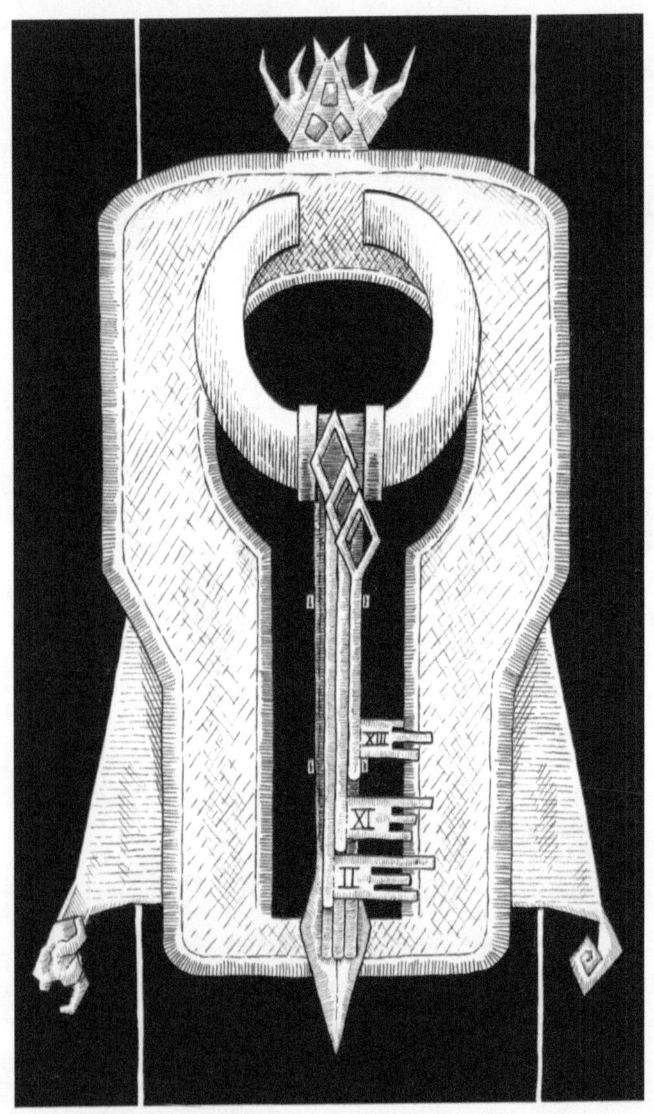

on the other side of that door. The door that will now be on the 'floor' of the enormous room. That if I open it with the keys, I wouldn't be walking out the door, I would have to climb out of it like climbing out of a hole. And, I explained, that there was a point in both the other rooms when I realized the world wasn't what I thought it was.

I pause to let him say something. Anything.

He stays quiet.

"But this time, I'm not sure," I say.

"How the fuck am I supposed to respond to you asking if I'm real, Echo," he asks.

"I'm not asking that. All I'm saying is that last night with my arm, with the dream —," I start.

He nods to push me to continue.

"It was the first time I felt like this place was surreal too," I say.

I tell him about the dreams. About him sanding me down, shaving pieces off me.

"It's just a dream," he says.

"I know, I know," I say. I hesitate to continue.

His brow furrows.

"You cannot be serious," he says.

"What?" I ask.

"Are you saying you think none of this is real? You think I'm not real?" His eyes meet mine as if from across a battlefield, my bowstring still vibrating with the release of an arrow.

"That's not exactly what I'm saying," I say, rushing the words out like children from a burning house.

He sighs.

"I'm not saying you aren't real. This isn't about you. I'm saying that here," I gesture at the couch we're sitting on, at the house around us, "I don't feel real."

His face softens. We sit. I wait.

"I've felt that way before," he says in a voice I've never heard. "Like the cat in the box. Alive and dead."

So succinct.

My abdomen tightens and my eyes well up.

We sit for a long time.

Next to each other for maybe the first time.

Day passes into evening which passes into night.

Without saying a word, he gets up and goes to the garage.

He comes back with a log for a fire.

Without saying a word, I head to the kitchen.

I return with two glasses of wine.

We sit back down on the couch, watch the fire log already crackling away in the fireplace, and sip our wine.

Before long, our glasses are empty and my head is on his shoulder.

"I'm in the box. Right now. I can't stay here forever," I whisper.

"It's risky," he says.

But his words mingle with understanding.

"I know you might not believe everything I told you this morning," I start.

He takes advantage of my pause.

"What do you need?" he asks my heart.

"I need to go back," I say.

"What does that look like for you?" he asks.

"Just —just opening the door," I say.

"Then tomorrow morning?" he asks.

"Tomorrow morning," I whisper.

We stay on the couch through the night, our hands and our hearts intertwined.

* * *

In the morning, he is still understanding, though stoic.

We fish the dog crate out of the attic and set it up against the back wall of the house. We push furniture against the wall and stack our lives around the crate to hold it in place.

We quietly tie sheets, pillowcases, and towels together to fashion a ladder. The sound of fabric against fabric, finding the best way to knot the different textures together. They smell fresh. They smell of lavender.

We drill brackets that had once hung in the garage onto the floor in front of the door. The whirling of the drill echoes in the foyer. We tie the ladder to the brackets.

We stand and brush the dust from our knees.

He puts his hand on my shoulder before drawing me in for a hug.

Once the dog is in her crate, I put on my jacket again.

The keys are in one pocket, the cotton and finger flasher in the other.

"Ready?" I ask.

He nods. I can't help but smirk at the doubt I still see in his eyes. I can't blame him.

We both secure our feet on the cloth ladder, giving it extra tugs to make sure it's secure.

I put my hand on the door handle and breathe deep.

The air rushes into my lungs like a flood.

I am more awake than I've ever been.

I open the door.

As if someone cut a rope bridge we were crossing, the room swings down and out from under us. We cling to the rope ladder and dangle below the door.

I struggle to let the door, heavy with gravity, swing open past me.

I look down to see the furniture still neatly stacked but laying on its side.

Annie, our dog, is safe in her crate.

My husband's eyes are wide.

I refocus and look up into the darkness.

I climb, slow and steady, trying to push my fear of heights from my mind.

Technically, you're still on the floor, I think.

Eventually, I pull myself up and onto the stone of the large room.

I shuffle to the side before looking back down into the house.

"Do you want to see?" I ask.

He says nothing but begins to climb.

He peeks his head up and out of the doorway.

"It's darker than I thought it would be," he says with a level of reverence I didn't expect.

"Me too," I admit.

Still standing on the ladder as if he knows he can't go any further, he looks around a little longer.

I look back at him to find his hand stretching toward mine.

I give him my hand and he squeezes it.

Then, he begins his descent back into the house.

He hoists the door toward me and meets my eye one last time.

We share one more moment of pain, grief, and understanding.

Then he pushes the door up toward me and I pull it closed from above.

I stand and look at the door on the floor once again from this abyss.

I feel it now. Deep and coursing through my veins.

Then I hear it.

It starts as a low growl, swirling around the edges of the room, emanating from the darkest places.

I'm not afraid.

I break into a run toward the far wall and the last door.

I see light from the few remaining torches in the tunnel jumping up onto the door above it. The tunnel, which now exists as a large hole in the floor between me and the door.

I'll have to unlock the door, push it open, and then jump into it.

I can do that.

I know now. This room is my last stop.

I'm less than a quarter of the way across the room when a gust of wind stronger than any of the others topples me backward and knocks the air out of me. A scream erupts into the darkness. I gasp for air, pull my knees to my chest, and cover my ears. The scream is so loud that my head is vibrating.

I'm left in silence with the ringing in my ears and a headache in my temples.

I push myself to my feet.

The gust extinguished the last of the torches in the tunnel, plunging me and the door into even deeper darkness.

It also means that this time, there actually is a large hole that I could fall into.

This is why the old woman gave me the finger flasher and the flash cotton.

I put my hands out in front of me and feel around with my foot before each step.

After I've walked at my turtle speed for some time, I decide it's time to do my first magic trick.

I only have enough flash cotton for two or three small bursts of light.

I load the small barrel and hold the toy above my head.

I click the ignition and the light comes and goes.

I feel the tension rise in my shoulders.

I'm not to the other side of the room yet.

But on the very edge of the small circle of light, I think I saw feet.

A figure standing just outside of my view.

Darkness playing tricks on the mind.

I keep moving even though my jaw is clenched so tight I can feel the pressure in my ears.

I inch what I hope is closer and closer to the other side of the room.

My outstretched hand brushes against something and I almost scream.

But it's just the wall.

I've made it to the other side.

I turn and put my back flat against it.

I didn't fall in the hole, but that also means I've missed the door.

After running my hands along the cool stone wall, I put my hand in my pocket and feel around for the flash cotton. I hold it in my hand, ripping it in half. I have enough for two more bursts.

I load the canister and hold it above my head once again.

I try to look around as quickly as I can during the split second of light.

I turn my head to the left and see the hole in the floor and I turn my head to the right.

There stands the figure, dressed in a dirty white nightgown, in bare feet. It is close enough that I can see it even after the light has gone. It has long dark hair and a broken jaw that hangs from its face, gently swinging side to side as it ambles toward me.

I force myself back into the moment and place my hands on the wall. If the thing was going to do something to me, I think it already would have. Taking one careful step at a time, I slide closer to the room, turning back to check what progress my quiet friend has made.

Finally, my hand slides from stone to a wooden doorframe.

I test the ground with my foot to see how close I am to the tunnel. As I find the edge with my foot, it fades into view in the darkness.

I check on the thing to the other side of me and my heart rate ramps up even higher, sending a surge of dizziness into my head.

It's nowhere to be seen.

There's a knot in my stomach.

I shove my hand into my pocket and pull out the keys. Of course, they've fallen apart. I scramble to put them back together. My hands are sweaty and shaking.

Finally, they all click into place.

I feel for the keyhole on the door and fumble to get the key in.

I finally hear it click twice. I'm able to swing the door open from my odd angle.

Then it's there again. Right in front of me, floating on what might have been the ground had the tunnel entrance not been below its feet.

It stands directly in my way.

Within arm's reach.

I have a thought. What if this thing isn't real?

I reach out to touch. My hand goes right through.

It screams the same blood-curdling scream I heard before. I cover my ears.

It keeps screaming. I take hold of the door frame and swing one foot in. With one more hop, I jump right through the thing and into the room, pushing the door closed behind me.

The screaming stops but I can still feel it. Still standing just outside the door.

I hear the door lock from the outside at the same time a match strikes behind me.

There is no doorknob on this side of the door, no visible hinges, no keyhole. Nothing.

I'm trapped.

Not ten inches from my face,

Once again,

Is me.

The back of the door is a pane of mirrored glass.

The light behind me illuminates my face.

I'm pale, covered in sweat, and have a brush burn on my cheek.

My eyes are bloodshot and wide.

My breathing is rapid and shallow.

I focus. I can't think about being stuck in here.

I'll stay aggressively present. My new favorite mantra.

Using the mirror, I look around the room.

It isn't just the door that's mirrored.

Every inch of all the walls and even the ceiling, all reflecting.

Each corner, like a vortex to another dimension.

The floor is made of large planks of wood.

In the middle of the room, there is a very small wooden table with a single white candle burning brightly.

Next to the table is a wooden chair.

There's no one in the room but me.

Me and my four reflections like four statues in the old woman's garden. But these are not my cardinal witches. These are more than my reflection.

My mind wanders to the bathroom mirror in the first house I ever lived in.

I would climb up onto the bathroom sink to fold the wings of the three-part mirror flush against my face, creating my own mirror room. I would look for hours, trying to see past myself, see the end of the mirror world. I did it so often that my mom would knock on the door and say, "Time to stop looking in the mirror."

I walk to the table with the candle on it. It looks as if it was just lit.

It's a tall, tapered candle in a brass candleholder. It looks old. The match used to light it is still in the base of the candleholder and the scent of the burning wick fills my nose.

I pick up the candle.

Something in my peripheral vision catches my attention.

I look around. Three sides of the mirror room show me holding the candle.

One does not.

I watch her as I set the candle down.

The other reflections disappear and she starts to clap her hands.

"You did it," she says. "You're here."

I don't say anything.

"You aren't supposed to be. But you're a stubborn thing, aren't you?"

She walks toward me. To what I imagine is the edge of her glass room. She puts her hand on the mirror.

"You're not going to say anything to me? Just gonna stand there?"

Silence.

She takes her hand down from the mirror and stares at me, hands on her hips.

She feels sorry for me. It's a face I've seen in the mirror before.

"Wanna see something cool?" she asks. Before I can reply she adds, "Look behind you."

This can't be good. I look over my shoulder.

She's on the other side of the room, happily waving to me.

"I'm fast!" she says, with obvious pride.

I turn back to the first wall to find her face an inch from mine.

"Boo," she says with a toothy Cheshire cat smile.

I scramble backward, knocking the table enough that I see the candle wobble.

We both try to catch it but we're too late.

The room is plunged into darkness.

I quietly sit down on the floor, bringing my knees to my chest. I will patiently wait for whatever may come.

I hear another match strike.

Through my eyelids, I see the orange haze of candlelight.

"You're boring," she says.

I open my eyes.

She's sitting on the wooden chair on the other side of the mirror, her arm resting on the table.

I get up before saying, "And you're an asshole."

The chair and table in my room once again match the ones in hers.

I walk to mine and sit down.

"She speaks!" she says, leaning forward. "So, are you scared of me?"

I think about it for a moment. "No."

Her smirk fades.

She uncrosses her arms and puts her hands on her knees.

Quickly, fluidly, she licks her fingers and places them on either side of the candle flame.

She waits for a reaction.

And gets none.

Her brow furrows and she douses the flame.

This time, I feel hugged by the darkness.

I welcome it as an old familiar friend.

A drawn-out whisper starts in my ear, so close that I can't tell if she's next to me or in my head, "What is fear, really?"

Then silence again.

I feel a cool breeze.

I'm tempted to look around in the dark but force myself to be still, even as the goosebumps pepper my skin.

BANG!

A deafening knock at the door.

I grab the seat of my chair as the shock settles in.

BANG!

BANG!

BANG!

Like claps of thunder, three more knocks.

I hear the handle on the outside jiggling, being pushed and pulled.

The darkness makes me feel like I'm closer to the door than I am.

Or am I closer than I remembered?

The doorknob jostles.

I reach my hand out toward the noise.

My eyes adjust to the darkness just in time to see my hand no more than an inch from the mirror.

I make contact with the door.

All goes silent. All but the quiet, ragged breathing just outside the door.

The door begins to shake like a barn door in a tornado.

BANG BANG,

BANG BANG.

Quick and strong, the chorus echoes around me.

The fear reignites in my gut as I wait for the mirrors to break.

I stand, unsure what else to do.

As soon as I reach my full height, the banging on the door is replaced by the whine of florescent lights.

Through squinted eyes, I find myself in a lecture hall.

I'm in one of the cavernous classrooms where they teach college foundation courses.

The two hundred or so seats are at least three-quarters full of students and the room is quiet.

I'm in the very middle of the room, standing at a desk.

I look down and see the bag I carried in college resting against my chair.

"Ma'am?" I hear.

All the students are looking at me.

I track the sound of the inquiry to the front of the hall where the professor is sitting with a quizzical look.

An older woman, her dark, frizzy hair framing her face.

"Did you have a question," she asks.

I glance around the classroom again before responding, "Uh, um, no."

The students laugh and continue to stare at me.

I take my seat.

"If you're going to disrupt my class, you'll have to leave," she says.

"Sorry… Professor," I say.

Then she's at my desk, standing so close to me that her hip almost bumps my shoulder.

I glance up at her torso, at her desk in the front of the room, and back at her.

The other students are all intently scribbling in their notebooks.

She's bending down now and as I look up, I am met with

Horror.

She has no face.

The smell of rotting flesh and infection fills my nose again.

The creature from the woods?

There are faint depressions and bumps where her facial features should be, but no openings.

She begins to struggle, clawing at her neck as if she can't breathe.

She blindly gropes around my desk, finding my pen. She plunges it into the space where her right eye should be.

I scream and the rest of the students scream with me but keep scribbling in their notebooks.

I stand and the students stand with me. Their notebooks stay on their desks, but their hands keep writing in midair.

The students, one by one, begin to move toward me.

They wave their pens like wands, eyes still concentrated on their invisible notebooks.

The Professor is still struggling on the ground behind me, blood pouring from her neck and three new holes she carved where her eyes and mouth should be.

I'm going to be sick.

The students, it now appears are not making their way toward me, but toward the professor.

The first student reaches her, his pen still writing in the air, until he too, plunges his pen into her neck. The next student reaches her and stabs her in the stomach.

I back away slowly.

I'm halfway to the door of the classroom when I bump into a chair. I hear the stabbing behind me pause.

I turn around to see all the students and the bloodied professor staring at me.

In unison, the students let out another scream.

I break into a run toward the door.

My first two steps are in the classroom, my third and fourth fall on the wooden floor of the mirrored room.

The candle is lit, she sits in her chair, her arms crossed in front of her.

"What the fuck?" I ask.

"It's my job," she says, with a smug smile.

"Your job?" I half ask, half scream.

She looks at me, incredulous. Then laughs.

"And what the fuck was that?" I ask, gesturing behind me even though the classroom is nowhere to be seen.

Her smile disappears.

I raise my eyebrows and shake my head.

"I keep you safe," she says, her face confused and solemn.

Again, I gesture behind me but with even more flourish.

"THAT is keeping me SAFE?" I ask.

"Are you afraid?" she asks.

"Yes!" I yell.

"Then yes," she says.

I can't stop shaking my head, trying to wrap my mind around the experiences of the past few minutes much less the past few days.

It's too much.

My reflection, now in the same room as me, leads me to the chair and I sit.

She takes my hands.

I don't pull away.

She kneels before me.

"After all you've been through, worked through, learned," she says, speaking in a patronizing, nurturing tone, "We made a deal and now, we stick with what we know."

I don't understand.

She pushes my hair behind my ear before continuing, "You know you won't be able to handle most things that get thrown at you. So, I keep you safe. That's why we like to be alone."

"If you know me at all, you know I hate being alone," I say.

She smiles a knowing smile, "You can be with people and still be alone, Echo. I make sure of that. You can't trust people. Come on, you know this. You're so *self-aware.*"

She holds my chin and smiles like she's proud of me.

I search her eyes. My eyes.

"Don't you see? You don't understand how the world works. You're a child. That's why I'm here. I remind you what safe is and where you can find it," she says.

Familiarity washes over me. I feel comforted by her words.

The seed is beginning to take root.

"I created you. When I was a little girl?" I ask.

"Not exactly. But I did come to be when you were quite young." she lets go of my hands.

"Were you with me in the woods?" I ask.

Her eyes light up, "Yes! I was with all of you in the woods."

"And in the garden?" I ask.

She turns her head like a dog that heard a strange sound.

Her brows furrow, "That's not how it works."

She lowers herself to the ground before me and lifts her hand to her head as if she has a headache.

I watch, waiting.

Nothing happens. I continue, "So, you weren't in the garden with me, then. So, who kept me safe there?"

"Where?" she asks.

"In the garden with the old woman?" I ask.

"I…," she starts, "The old woman… she's not mine."

"I don't understand," I say.

My reflection is now visibly distressed. Sweat speckles her forehead. "The little girl existed before me. The old woman—"

"Exists after you." I finish her sentence. The first sprout of understanding is peeking its head out of the soil.

She shifts uncomfortably. I might not have noticed if we weren't the same person. She meets my gaze.

"Oh my god. You. You are afraid!" I say in amazement.

"Don't be disrespectful," she says, standing up.

"Stop," I say. I stand too.

The density of the air changes along with something in her face.

"What are you doing?" she asks.

Before I can answer, she's pushed backward, back through the glass.

She places her hand on the glass as if she can't believe what just happened. To my surprise, she smiles.

"You forget who I am," she says.

She snaps and the candle goes out.

We are back in darkness.

My patience grows thin and I whisper, "Get on with it."

Before I even finish my mutter, I hear a click.

Like an interrogation lamp switched on above my head, it's so bright that all I can see is white.

I cover my head with my arms in response.

I squint through my arms and see that I'm still in the room but the walls are no longer mirrors. They're now just glass panes.

I feel like a creature on display.

The glass box is now in the middle of the large stone room.

I look around the room but see nothing.

Then I see her. She's walking toward me from the far wall, from the dark.

Just before she reaches the glass pane, another me emerges behind her.

She also slowly, methodically approaches the glass.

Then another.

And another.

They started filing out faster and faster until the glass panes are completely lined, and three-deep with… me.

All smiling.

Still a step away from the glass, they all stare.

I can feel their eyes creeping over my skin.

The light overhead dims as do their smiles.

It triggers a memory of sleepovers when you stay up late giggling with your best friend and then their mom comes in and says it's time to turn off the light. But you have far too many pressing issues to discuss so you stay up even after it's dark. I'm reminded of that moment when the conditions are just right and you stare at your friend's face just a little too long and it begins to turn a little ghoulish.

Just on the edge of the light stand dozens of transitioning faces.

Faces I know turning into faces I wished I could forget.

Just before the light goes out, I hear the murmur of feet on stone.

The bodies converge on the glass.

They all start screaming and pounding on the glass, no longer trying to scare me.

They're trying to get in. They are afraid.

There's a new presence.

Or an old one.

Moving from the darkest corner of the stone room toward the glass box.

The faceless woman from the classroom floats toward the glass box. Blood runs down her body, flowing from her open wounds.

As she approaches, the others become manic.

One by one, they're torn down until I'm no longer surrounded by screams, but the piercing silence of bodies piled on the floor.

Somewhere, outside the glass, she's waiting for me.

I feel a hand on my shoulder and as I begin to scream, I feel another hand clamp over my mouth.

It is my reflection.

She's telling me to be silent.

I struggle against her grip.

She whispers with haste, "Please," she says, "please, stay still. Stay quiet. She'll find us, she'll find us!"

I'm ready, I think.

I wriggle a hand free and shove it into my pocket.

I manage to get the flash cotton into the canister while the toy is still in my pocket.

With all my strength, I push her arms off me and hold my hand high.

I click the ignition but instead of a small explosion, an enormous fireball erupts from my hands, shattering the glass box. It floats upward until it meets the ceiling and then hangs there like a giant chandelier.

"No!" I hear my reflection yell from somewhere behind me. "You don't understand!"

Her voice fades as does the sound of her footsteps running away.

The faceless woman approaches. Her hair softly flows around where her face should be.

She stops a few feet in front of me.

The scent is less overwhelming than it had been in the woods.

I look at her throat and the place where her eyes should be.

In the luminescence of the fireball, I see her bloodied body is malnour-ished.

I feel pity for her.

She reaches a hand toward me.

I take it.

We are transported to the roof of a building.

The sun is setting and the view is beautiful.

I walk to the railing.

The woman stands beside me. She waves her hand toward the horizon.

From her pocket, she brings out a needle and thread.

She hands them to me and motions toward her eyes.

I don't feel inclined to take them but she did help the child when I ran away. Even if it was misguided, that must mean something.

She continues to hold the needle and thread toward me in good faith that I will take it.

I do.

In the sunset, on top of this building, the building I built to house all my emotions in their separate rooms, on their separate floors, I sew Shame's eyes shut.

"Can you heal?" I ask her.

Without fear bubbling in my belly, her voice is much more tender than it had sounded in the woods.

"I cannot," she says. "But you can."

A door flies open behind us. My reflection races toward us.

"Echo, no! You don't understand! You don't know who this is," says my reflection.

"She is Shame," I say.

"You know and yet you follow her? She is everything that is wrong with the world, little girl," she says. "You don't understand. You can't."

Before I can react, she pushes me. Hard.

The railing presses into my back as my feet leave the floor.

Panic courses through my veins as I flip over the railing and begin to fall.

At the last possible second, I feel a hand around my wrist.

I hold on for dear life.

"Don't you see?" says my reflection. "You need me! You would fall without me here."

"You pushed me!" I yell back at her.

She lets go of my wrist but I am still holding onto her.

"You hold onto me, sweet girl. Not the other way around."

My eyes fill with tears.

As I dangle there, I glance out over the horizon and see the dusk settling in over the skyline.

Still holding on, I look up.

"You have kept me safe. I know that. And you," I look at Shame, "You have been the only place I was able to be myself for so long. But I don't need you anymore. I am safe. This building comes down today."

I close my eyes and take a deep breath.

"I'll remember you both. Always."

I look at the horizon once more.

I feel the vibrations and hear the building start to crumble.

I let go.

* * *

My feet make contact, not a foot below where they dangled.

I fall to the ground and am surrounded by dandelions and forget-me-nots.

I look around and see an evening sun casting golden light on the green swaying grass.

I'm in the clearing.

I look at my hands. They're clean.

I feel my cheek, no brush burn.

My skin feels warm as if I'd napped in a sunny field all day.

I find the trailhead right in the place that it's always been.

I follow it out of the woods and back to the road.

Just before my feet reach the pavement, I stop.

There's something underfoot.

I look down and see a single white rose on the ground.

I pick it up

And put it in my hair.

HOME

Hope

I needed you
I needed something more
I needed your heart
Your very soul

I needed to feel
You needing me
I needed more

And you gave it.
Freely.
Thank you.

I Swear

A flower blooms inside.
Goosebumps, eyes wide.
Their origin, unknown.
Like a garden overgrown,
These unruly emotions
Causing a commotion.
I am light, I am aware,
Like a burst of fresh air!
Out of darkness, I strut
For I no longer give a fuck.

Ah, Youth

Youth is so pretty
So shiny.
But age and wisdom,
They glow

Love

It's on the nose like a freckle,
On the porch like a rocking chair,
In the garden like a swing,
On the water like a wave.
I spend so much time
Looking for love in other arms
Forgetting that my love is inherent.
Present, calm, beautiful, and deep,
And mine. A love all my own.
The love I can call home.

Planted

I feel them deep and growing.
Pushing past soil and rock.
There's strength found in knowing
There is no time, no clock.
I hear the earth's expression
As down and down they reach
Force through the compression
With every inch, they teach.
Slowly slither and crawl,
They dig and dig for water.
And I stand firm and tall.
Mother Nature's daughter.

Taraxacum Officinale (Pissenlit)   Pl. XXII.

Careful

Never underestimate
your ability to hope.
Be wary.
It'll fill your head with notions
and your heart with yearning.

State of Mind

I finally feel at home.
Between these wooden walls.
I found within myself
A cavernous hope.
And there, I hang my hat.
There, I rest my head.

Here

Sometimes poems are about something.
Sometimes they sing, sometimes they sting.
Sometimes there's a lesson to learn or a storyline.
Sometimes they rhyme.
Sometimes they don't.
Sometimes they're written in stanzas.
Sometimes they're written in couplets.
Sometimes they make no sense.
Sometimes they make sense ten years after you read them.
And sometimes they don't tell you anything besides
What's in my head at this very moment.
And then we're together.
For just a few seconds, we shared this thought.
And it was beautiful.
Let's meet here whenever we're lonely.

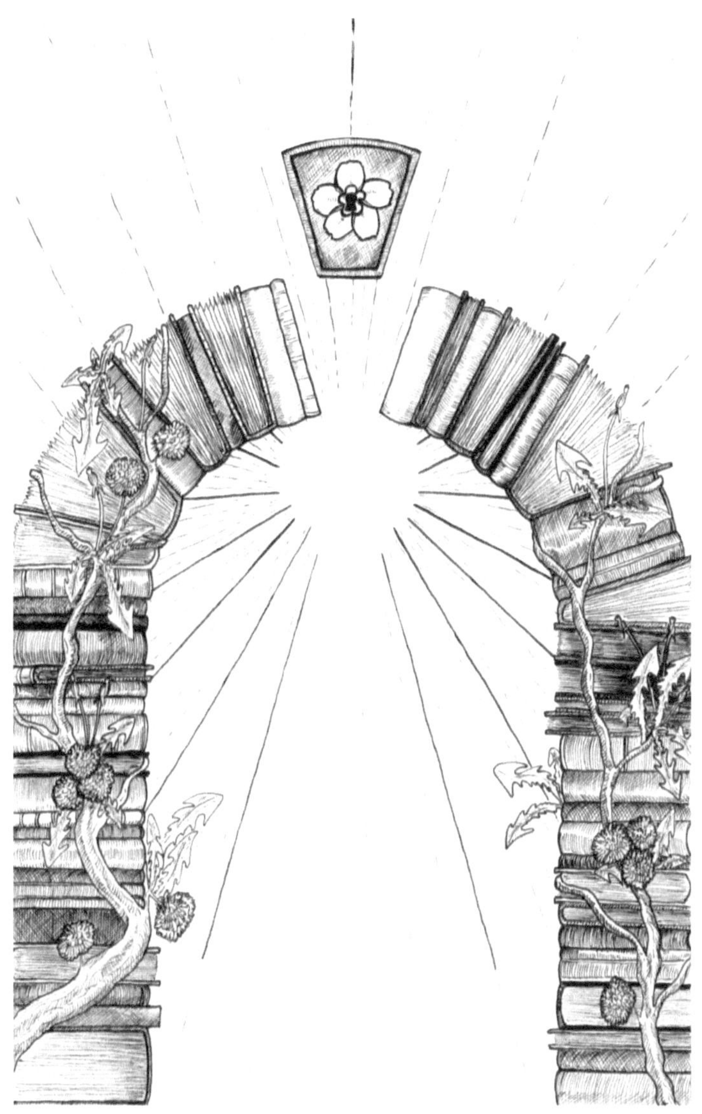

Content Warnings

Some of these warnings are literal but many are metaphorically referenced at different intervals during the story parts and/or poems.

Literal:

Blood
Gore
Mental Health
Swearing
Tarot
Vomit

Metaphorical:

Guilt
Emotional Abuse
Childhood Sexual Abuse
Religious Trauma
Sexuality
Shame

Inspirations and Healing

THE following list will probably seem like a mishmash of unrelated media. But to me, this list was my path through the woods that led me to and through the wall. I may not agree with every single word in the following selections, but I will say that each item on this list helped me overcome something I needed to overcome in order to finish this project and to live a fuller life. These things helped me to see myself more clearly and eroded fears that I thought were integral to who I was. But I was wrong. And I will be eternally grateful to everyone and everything on this list and many, many more. Thank you for being a source of knowledge, understanding, genius, and curiosity.

*Note: These citations are far from perfect. And some are downright terrible.

Short Stories

Dowling, T. (2003). One thing about the night. In E. Datlow (Ed.), The dark: new ghost stories (pp. 63-82). Tom Doherty Associates, LLC., New York.

Podcasts

Boyd, R. & Rhoads, Q. (2017-2021). Rank and vile podcast.

Price, J. (2018-2021). The sacred speaks podcast.

Horror Books

Leiber, F. (1943). Conjure wife. Street & Smith Publications.

Jackson, S. (1959). The haunting of hill house. Viking Publisher.

Shelley, M. (1818). Frankenstein. Lackington, Hughes, Harding, Mavor & Jones.

Shows and Movies

Kripke, E. & Singer, R. (Producers). (2005-2020). Supernatural. Warner Bros. Television Distribution.

Gracey, M. (Director). (2017). The Greatest Showman. 20th Century Fox.

Buzzfeed Unsolved Supernatural with Ryan Bergera and Shane Madej (now owners of the Watcher Network on YouTube with Stephen Lim)

Myth

Miller, M. (2018). Circe. Little, Brown and Company, New York.

Pinkola Estés, C. (1995). Women who run with the wolves: myths and stories of the wild woman archetype. Random House, New York.

Books That Healed

Bass, E., & Davis, L. (1988). The courage to heal: A guide for women survivors of child sexual abuse. Perennial Library/Harper & Row Publishers, New York.

Beattie, M. (1992). Codependent no more: how to stop controlling others and start caring for yourself (2nd ed.). Hazelden Publishing, Minnesota.

Bidwell, D.R. (2018). When one religion isn't enough: the lives of spiritually fluid people. Beacon Press, Massachusetts.

Brown, B. (2010). The gifts of imperfection: let go of who you think you're supposed to be and embrace who you are. Hazelden Publishing, Minnesota.

Brown, B. (2017). Braving the wilderness: the quest for true belonging and the courage to stand alone. Random House, New York.

Bradshaw, J. (2005). Healing the shame that binds you. Health Communications, Inc., Florida.

Haidt, J. (2012). The righteous mind: why good people are divided by politics and religion. Vintage Books/Random House, New York.

Harris, T.A. (1969). I'm ok – you're ok. Harper, New York.

Jampolsky, G.G. (1970). Love is letting go of fear. Bantam Books, New York.

Kenner, C. (2009). Tarot for Writers. Llewellyn Publications, Minnesota.

Kreger, R & Mason, P.T. (2010). Stop walking on eggshells: taking your life ack when someone you care about has borderline personality disorder (2nd ed.). New Harbinger Publications.

Kripal, J.J. (2019). The flip: epiphanies of mind and the future of knowledge. Bellevue Library Press, New York.

Lerner, H. (2014). The dance of anger: a woman's guide to changing patterns in intimate relationships. HarperCollins, New York.

Lerner, H. (1990). The dance of intimacy: a woman's guide to courageous acts of change in key relationships. Harper Perennial, New York.

Mellody, P., Miller, A.W., & Miller, K. (2003). Facing codependence: what it is, where it comes from, how it sabotages our lives. Harper & Row.

Moulton Sarkis, S. (2018). Gaslighting. Da Capo Lifelong Books.

Orloff, J. (2017). The empath's survival guide: life strategies for sensitive people. Sounds True, Colorado.

Pert, C.B. (1997). Molecules of emotion: the science behind mind-body medicine. Touchstone/Simon & Schuster, New York.

Roth, B. (2018). Strength in stillness: the power of transcendental meditation. Simon & Schuster, New York.

Ruiz, D.M. (2018). The four agreements. Amber-Allen Publishing.